ENL

Intimacy is the purpose, poss⸻ ⸻ ⸻⸺
resurrection. *The Posture Princ*, ⸺ ⸺⸺⸺ us to this quest. It provokes us to
embrace the unbelievable status and supernatural experience of being sons
and daughters of God. I can put it no better than Martina does: 'Unexpected
Warriors are those who do not win by strength, fame or qualification. They
win, because Jesus won for them, and they have been set free to become the
real children of God they were created to be.'

**Mark Iles**
*School for Prophecy*

I am a great believer in the power of our beliefs, therefore I highly recommend
Martina Davis' *The Posture Principle*. This book will equip with the beliefs
and attitudes of the heart that will position you to receive the fullness of who
we are and what God has for us.

**Steve Backlund**
*Associate Leader/Pastor Bethel Church of Redding, California*

I found Martina's ability to speak in laymen's terms refreshing. She manages
to link Scripture with the everyday and tell a story that excites our imagination and faith to believe that this is really what the Word can do. It comes
from a deep place and describes where she is.

**Jane Coburn**
*lay visitor, All Saints, Swanage*

The book carries an impartation to have deeper personal intimacy, dialogue,
and encounters with God built on kingdom foundation. Martina, you are a
releaser of kairos moment breakthroughs and mindset shifts. Many people
will be set free from years of struggle or oppression by your testimony/book
as you walk people through building the right foundation for deep intimacy
with God and seeing Him rightly as an extravagant Father.

**Michelle Moon**
*Third Year to Sarah Gerber, Igniting Hope Ministries*

This is a very practical book on spiritual living.

**Paul Stanier**
*Zaccmedia*

# THE
# POSTURE
# PRINCIPLE

Book 1
THE EQUIPPING UNEXPECTED
WARRIORS SERIES

# Martina Davis

 Zaccmedia

Published by Zaccmedia
www.zaccmedia.com
info@zaccmedia.com

Published December 2017

ISBN: 978-1-911211-71-6

British Library Cataloguing-in-Publication Data
A catalogue record for this book is available from the British Library.

Zaccmedia aims to produce books that will help to extend and build up the Kingdom of God. We do not necessarily agree with every view expressed by the authors, or with every interpretation of Scripture expressed. We expect readers to make their own judgment in the light of their understanding of God's Word and in an attitude of Christian love and fellowship.

Cover photo copyright © 2017 Martina Davis, Author
From her painting entitled 'More'.

We are born to make the dark places afraid by love.
We have a different Spirit.

*Martina Davis*

# CONTENTS

## THE POSTURE PRINCIPLE

*What you value most, you will protect.*

## WEEK ONE: FOCUS

*Fix your eyes on Him. Take time to gaze, to look, to think, as He meets you where you are.*

## WEEK TWO: ESTABLISHING

*Know the depths of the grace of the Lord Jesus, the heights of the love
of the Father, and the width of the wisdom from the Holy Spirit,
in your life!*

## WEEK THREE: FINISHING

*Finish well, close to the heartbeat of God in partnership with Him,
empowered by His Spirit and full of His peace.*

# ACKNOWLEDGEMENTS

THANK YOU,

To my husband Richard, our life together is treasure to me.

To our sons James and David, being your mother has been a joyous adventure!

To our son Robert, see you in heaven where we'll have a good catch-up.

To the churches that became my family wherever we travelled while in the army, you were my seedbed.

To my mentor and spiritual father, Mark Iles, who consistently shows me a fresh relationship with my heavenly Father.

To Steve and Wendy Backlund and the team at Bethel Church, California, who have been hope-igniters, joy-releasers, fathers and mothers to me; and Michelle Moon who reviewed my manuscript.

To my fellow School for Prophecy members, you represent the diversity of Father's creation.

To my book midwives, Emma, Jane, Jane, Rebeca, Janet and Elaine.

To Paul Stanier of Zaccmedia and to Sheila Jacobs my editor.

To my God, who made me and loves me.

# FOREWORD

It is always satisfying to watch someone who is taking back their biblical inheritance in Christ that was stolen from them, and this book represents the declaration of that journey for Martina. The grace measure in our lives is how far we have come, and not how far we have to go. In this book, Martina profoundly, powerfully and practically declares that truth, and honestly and vulnerably gives the glory to Jesus. Martina's experience has brought her to this place, which she openly shares with us.

This book is birthed in and specifically reflects Martina's journey and life to this point. It demonstrates the embracing of core biblical principles and the discovery of her true identity in Christ. It reflects her journey breaking free from performance, religion, lies and ungodly culture. I wholeheartedly support this because my experience has taught me that the majority of our problems are due to a lack of understanding of what Jesus accomplished on the cross. She has remarkably used our physical backbone as an allegory for unlocking the deep spiritual truth of intimacy with our heavenly Father.

This book is unusual. It is not a textbook or a novel, but neither is it a workbook. It is an inspirational guide-book that walks you through a three-week meditation focused on the core biblical value of 'intimacy'. Martina knows I will enjoy the alliteration she has employed in the daily meditations, as this is a well-known part of my teaching style. It is undoubtedly a book 'For such a time as this' (Esther 4:14) and seeks to empower us to embrace our true calling in these challenging times.

I am pleased to see the practical exercises included after each day's inspirational meditation. It has been a particular emphasis of mine to make sure what I share is accessible, applicable and activating, and the daily exercises achieve this objective. The repetition each day of the posture, stopping, breathing, relaxation and soaking keys enhance this whole process. The practical nature of this book helpfully addresses the question 'Can these bones live?' and guides us into a deeper intimacy with God through our posture revealing our treasure.

One of the most significant aspects of this book is that it is specifically and accurately aimed at the poor in spirit (Matthew 5:3). It is wonderfully targeted at those the world has written off but who suddenly find themselves smelling and tasting Christ's victory. This book echoes the Isaiah 61 ministry we have inherited from Jesus, to proclaim good news to the poor. It confronts the world's value system because God has chosen the things that are not, to nullify the things that are (1 Corinthians 1:28).

Intimacy is the purpose, possibility and proclamation of Jesus' death and resurrection. *The Posture Principle* calls us to this quest. It provokes us to embrace the unbelievable status and supernatural experience of being sons and daughters of God. I can put it no better than Martina does: 'Unexpected Warriors are those who do not win by strength, fame or qualification. They win, because Jesus won for them, and they have been set free to become the real children of God they were created to be.'

*Mark Iles*
*School for Prophecy*

# THE WARRIOR CALL

We had no voice; God gives us a voice to declare freedom. We despaired; God lights a fire of hope within us. Religion was our father; God our Creator comes close, as our true, loving, Father God and we become His sons and daughters.

Unexpected Warriors are those who do not win by strength, fame or qualification. They win, because Jesus won for them, and they have been set free to become the real children of God they were created to be. They daily use weapons that are not of this world, that seem soft, but are packed full of resurrection power, power to raise people from the dead to live lives to set others free. They win, by standing.

Unexpected Warriors are also those who never expected to have a voice. They are those who were hidden, but who have come to light. They have been lit by the touchpaper of God, breathed into by His breath so that they discover who they really are.

Martina Davis, July 2017

# PREFACE

## EQUIPPING UNEXPECTED WARRIORS

*For though we live in the world, we do not wage war as the world does. The weapons we fight with are not the weapons of the world.*
*2 Corinthians 10:3-4a*

Warriors of Light bring light. They preach good news to the poor, they bind up the broken-hearted. They proclaim freedom for the captives, and release from darkness for the prisoners.[1] They fight daily as children of the King who has already won the war, as stealth warriors, divinely demolishing strongholds, arguments, pretensions and capturing every thought to Christ.[2]

Those who reached the end of themselves but rose again know what I am talking about when I say there are

---

1   See Isaiah 61:1.

2   See 2 Corinthians 10:4b-5.

those of us who never expected to be counted amongst 'Warriors'. We were in valleys of defeat, and much of that was due to wrong beliefs about God; lack of understanding of our identity; religion, lies and a performance culture, all causing our captivity.

That is why I am writing this series of three books, on Posture, Identity and Freedom.

At five years old, fifty years ago, a little girl was creating a colouring of Jesus as King of kings. She met Him at that point, and received an understanding that did not emerge until much later. Jesus, seated royally on His horse, colourful mantle flowing and golden jewel-inlaid crown, was carrying a sword, yet the words she wrote above His head were these: 'Jesus is my Friend. He has put His name upon me. Jesus is King of all KINGS!' with the letters steadily growing bigger. The picture in its folder now is as bright as it ever was then, just a little crinkled and coffee-stained. It was mine.

It describes a relationship where we know Jesus as King and yet we know Him as a Friend and we carry His authority as the Father's children, and a Bride. Not an easy concept for a five-year-old.

What, after all, is that authority, that name upon us, for? In these short books I want to open our eyes and help us to think about what we need to do to understand and move into our full authority, identity, and freedom.

# INTRODUCTION

## THE POSTURE PRINCIPLE

This short book has emerged out of a five-year personal voyage, through two completed manuscripts, to reach this format, with this message, at this point of time.[3]

There have been large pauses, when I have known the hand of God working in my life to shape what He needed to before this was produced.

I present a message and a voice, for such a time as this, when prophetic people need to run long, true and real, without hype. We need to be transparent and wise.

Our Posture, Identity and Freedom are subjects we will examine in this series. This first book on our 'Posture' looks at ourselves as spirit, soul and body. We are positioning the whole of ourselves to receive all that God has

---

3  Check out Esther 4:14.

for us. Our posture, our attitude of heart will be, in the long run, what enables us to establish deep identity and lasting freedom in our lives, which is why it comes first.

I have laid out *The Posture Principle* as a three-week meditational study, intending to provoke you to think and to mull things over. You do not have to agree – my intention is to help you to seek God, find Him, chat to Him, and experience Him. After all, Warriors think for themselves, decide what to believe and what will drive their life.

You will be uncovering what you count as most important in your life, and therefore how you determine to position yourself from now on. Your 'posture' will reveal your treasure.

I have also used some keys to activate your body, soul and spirit, in the daily activities.

I have deliberately not interpreted the allegory so that you will need to spend time with it and ask the Holy Spirit to help you see how it might speak to you.

There are references to parts of our spine, to illustrate my points. I have learned these things through visits to my physiotherapist for treatment, which is how I have experienced in stark detail the extent to which our spirit, soul and body affect one another. Yet we overcome! God is a miracle-working God, and I have been on the receiving end of miracles, as well as being the vehicle for them to occur in the lives of others.

I use the illustration of the woman who poured perfume onto Jesus throughout this book. She could let go of things that other people could not.

My prayer is this, that you be taken into intimate times with the Father, where you will be able to talk about what He thinks of you, what you think, and what matters most to you both. That you'll be drawn towards hearing what the key treasure is in your life, to understanding how doing things that are contrary to your natural inclination of preserving your time, your reputation, and your influence, actually preserve your treasure, and even increase all that you sought to protect. That this book helps you find answers to pressing questions. What do you value most? How do you protect that? What are you willing to fight for and how? Where have you come from? Where are you going?

# PROLOGUE

## CAN THESE BONES LIVE?

'CAN THESE BONES LIVE?' I sensed God ask me on 23 May 2014. Then I saw and heard the following:

I see dry bones gathering together in the valley of defeat. These are people. As they gather they are coming alive and they go into the nation; they take their places and stand. As they do, a touchpaper lights them and they become torches of flame that light other dry bones around them; those then stand up and they form an army of a new generation, formed to follow God's purposes, and to fulfil them on the earth.

There are marathon runners amongst this group of people. These will have endurance and speed. They will be in for the long haul and will need to train. They will know their run in every detail, they will picture every turn, every step, in their minds so that when it comes time to run they will run with knowledge, accuracy, speed and ability. They will carry torches.

I saw little lights shooting in curves over to other continents, and then they shot back again. These are the light bringers. They need a base to be brightened each time they return.

I saw that each one has their own way of bringing life, of bringing the bones to life, and breathing the breath into them. It is important to hear what breath we have, and to increase it.

Increase it! Because Father is blowing across the land, blowing across the nation, He is blowing His breath across the nation, and He is bringing the people to kneel before Him in righteousness and justice which is His throne; He will build His throne upon us, and it will be seen that we are Glory-carriers.

These flame-carriers are going to need to go out filled, and worship is going to be key. They will need to know the Father, really know the Father in a Father-son relationship, being favoured carriers of inheritance.

There will be a new Spirit that rises up in us, and we will laugh – there is going to be an explosion of joy. Throughout those places where the flames are taken, bones will be shaken, not with terror, but by laughter. As they are shaken, the flesh will build on them and the muscle and sinew, and they will find new talents and skills because their fingers are working, and their feet will walk. Their hearts will be lifted and they will be proclaimers of the deeds of God, and the presence of God. This will be a movement that touches the lowliest; in fact where the lowliest are, they will become the highest. The highest will lower themselves to serve them, and to serve the Lord.

# THE POSTURE PRINCIPLE

## WHAT YOU VALUE MOST,
## YOU WILL PROTECT.

### Structure

In this book, I talk about an important section of our spiritual backbone: Intimacy with God.

In the physical body, the thoracic spine is one of three sections of our backbone,[4] and its role and positioning is crucial in the movement and function of our body.

Without the intimate relationship with God – Father, Son and Holy Spirit – each of these spiritual vertebrae in this crucial section of 'spine' will be out of line, causing strain and lack of freedom for the whole 'body'. This will have repercussions not only in our spirit, but also in soul and body.

---

4   Three sections of the spine are explained later, under *'Bones'*.

I have chosen twelve 'vertebrae' that I consider form our spiritual thoracic spine, depending on our attitude towards them. Each 'vertebra' begins with a 'P' which is deliberate, to help you remember.

We will look at each 'vertebra' in turn, and I will use the illustration of the woman in the Bible who poured perfume over Jesus throughout this book, as well as other specific characters, as meditation, giving thought and consideration to them to straighten and develop the health of these areas in our lives.

There are opportunities given in each chapter, to put into practice disciplines I have learned on my journey with physiotherapy, and throughout my life, all or some of which may be of help to you at various times of your own life.

The book is set out into three weeks, each week with four days of these short meditational studies and exercises. On days five and six of each week, I suggest an activity to strengthen what you have learned. The seventh day is for rest.

The study weeks are entitled: 1. FOCUS, 2. ESTABLISHING, and 3. FINISHING.

## 1. Week One: FOCUS

I believe that as we focus our attention upon how we see, and how we define, the four top vertebrae of Possibility, Purpose, Potential and Provision, we will begin to understand what God has prepared for us who love Him, that God has revealed to us by His Spirit.[5] Our sights will be lifted. Our hope will be recharged or reignited. And we will have spent time looking carefully into God's face to see truth in Him. These vertebrae in the physical body support the top part of the spine which is the neck, on which our head turns! From that we can look, and focus. This is also at the top of our ribcage.

## 2.   Week Two: ESTABLISHING

Here, we move to establish our focus. We find the next four vertebrae, which have ribs attached, protect our heart and lungs. Meditating on Protection brings a security. Preparation brings a heart of rest that God is in charge and is moving on our behalf. We receive and speak His Promises over our lives as we establish ourselves in the Scriptures and move about our day. We find strength, fight and stand, establishing our ground by holding to the Prophecies spoken over our lives that we have tried and tested, in which we have faith.[6]

---

5   See 1 Corinthians 2:9-10.

6   For comprehensive, clear, teaching on Prophecy and our handling of it, contact Mark Iles, *School for Prophecy* (see Resources to connect). Two Manuals are due publishing: Mark Iles, *Developing Your Prophetic Gift,*

### 3. Week Three: FINISHING

As we race towards the finishing line in our lives and in these studies, these last four vertebrae, which also have ribs attached protecting our internal organs, bring a sense of consistency and perseverance. Notice they are flexible enough with connecting ligaments, tendons and muscles, to expand with the breath we breathe. We cannot finish without the Holy Spirit in grace, in our Partnership and Pursuing. Power is required and Peace seals the victory.

## Experience

You could say that these 'vertebrae', without intimacy with God, become 'dry bones'[7] that need life breathed into them – a great relationship with their Creator God. Yet an intimate relationship is only possible with good beliefs about God and His character, and it grows through experience of Him, not intellectual learning about Him.

Although identity is given to us when we commit our lives to Jesus – we gain a new DNA, we are a new

---

*School for Prophecy Level 1 Manual* (Onwards and Upwards, due Spring 2018); Mark Iles, *Growing A Prophetic Ministry, School for Prophecy Level 2 Manual* (due for publishing 2019). Also see Kris Vallotton, *Basic Training for the Prophetic Ministry* (Destiny Image, 2014).

7   Ezekiel 37:2.

creation, we are children of God, we are in a new family – it can take a while before that is understood in our hearts, and outworked in our lives. That is why 'Identity' is the second book in the series, and 'Posture' the first. In looking at our beliefs and attitudes, we will see how we need to adjust our position to receive the fullness of our identity, long-term.

Attitudes, which are thoughts plus attached emotions, affect our physical bodies.[8] Our mind is the battleground upon which we fight lies and preconceptions. Beliefs form our thoughts, and good beliefs give us the eyes, and weapons, with which to recognise and protect our mind from the lies.[9] Bad attitudes come out of toxic thinking, due to faulty beliefs about God. We are told to take our thoughts captive to Jesus Christ,[10] and that is a key part of our 'Warrior' training.[11] It takes time and effort.

Posture is a way of life, how you sit, walk, stand, run, lift and do any form of physical exercise. Faulty posture sets up chain reactions through our bodies, which if it

---

8    Dr Caroline Leaf, *Switch On Your Brain* is a great resource (Baker, 2015).

9    Recommended teaching on these areas can be found in the above *School for Prophecy* courses and manuals, on Steve Backlund's website ignitinghope. com, in Joyce Meyer's book *Battlefield of the Mind* (Hodder & Stoughton Ltd 1995).

10    2 Corinthians 10:4-5.

11    'The only instruction that is given for how to pull down strongholds is the "capturing" of every lying thought.' Steve Backlund, *Cracks in the Foundation* (Steve Backlund, 2014).

goes uncorrected, causes damage to soft tissue (muscles, ligaments, tendons), and bones. Internal organs can also be affected – for instance, lungs being given less space to expand within the chest, or the digestive system becoming cramped.

One key area affects all the others, and that is what is named by my physiotherapist as the 'lordosis'. This is the natural inward curve in the lumbar spine, below the area we are speaking about. Often we sit hunched, with the curve rounded outwards and collapsed. This is usually because our core muscles are not supporting us, due to their weakness. Yet if our core is strong, then we can retain that curve and then the rest of our body can fall into line. Our shoulders drop and our upper body becomes more relaxed. This usually requires a fair amount of practice, a good diet and exercise of our core muscles!

I call that curve 'leaning on God'. Relationship with Him is at our core. We are told, 'Trust in the LORD with all your heart and lean not on your own understanding; in all your ways submit to him, and he will make your paths straight' (Proverbs 3:5-6). He brings a peace, a relaxation, a rest, to our whole spiritual posture.

During my own journey, due to my own experience, for periods of time I have had to learn to break every twenty minutes during the day, particularly when sitting at my desk. This is an enormous discipline! Particularly at the times when feeling no pain, as there was nothing to push me to stop. It is hard when engrossed in something to break off. Yet this helped me learn to discipline my mind, will and emotions as well as be refreshed and refocussed, in spirit and body, as I began to use this time well.

## Bones

To set the scene, I need to give a short overview of the physical structure of our spine. There are three flexible areas of the spine, and from top to bottom they are: the cervical spine, thoracic spine, and lumbar spine.

In *The Posture Principle* I speak of the thoracic spine, a stretch of twelve vertebrae which travels from the base of the neck to the base of the ribcage.

This thoracic spine is crucial for a range of movements, being built for rotation, flexion and extension. Not only that, but pairs of rib bones extend from the spaces between the twelve vertebrae. These rib bones form a structure that protects vital organs such as the heart and lungs. Each vertebra has a disc between it, but also has facet joints where it moves against the facet joints of the next vertebra, and the ribs.

All these joints and bones are intricately connected to ligaments, muscle and other tissue running in all directions. This means that when there is tension in any muscle or ligament for a long time, this can pull on the joints and the joints become stiffened and out of alignment. Obviously, the longer this is the case, the more stiffness and damage ensues.

For a healthy alignment to be restored, physiotherapy to loosen first the joints and then the soft tissue, along with disciplined, consistent, movement, exercise and stretching is required. Posture correction, and core strengthening are also needed. Sometimes we discover that we have also been walking and moving in a certain way that has put strain on the wrong muscles, or that we have damaged the area through overuse.

## Extravagance

At the beginning of this chapter I highlighted that our spiritual backbone is intimacy with God.

As we begin our three weeks, I want us to take time to let our minds wander avenues they have not yet fully explored, renew our thinking and begin, or continue, the adventure of listening to your Father in heaven who desires that we understand His passion for us first and foremost. Come awake to what matters most!

The question is, what do you value most? This will determine your posture in life. Just as the backbone carries the body, so what we value supports our lives.

The woman with the alabaster jar of perfume who anointed Jesus, saw life with very different eyes to the disciples. Her values brought her peace, Jesus' support and affirmation, and a legacy that reached into eternity in every person to whom the gospel was to be brought.[12]

12  Matthew 26:6-16; Mark 14:1-11; read also Luke 7:36-50.

Her act was quite opposite to what was expected, because of what she held most highly. For that she was criticised by the disciples, because the money from selling the perfume could have fed the poor. We see that Judas felt so strongly about it because he habitually stole from their collection, and her act was the prompt he needed to go to the chief priests to ask what they were willing to give him if he were to deliver Jesus to them. Our values can draw out criticism even from those closest to us. Yet our values keep our posture!

We have been told that we are living in a world to which we do not belong, as citizens of the heavenly Kingdom. As a result, we will experience resistance, misunderstanding, and difficulties.[13] Jesus promised that He would always be with us, but He did not promise an easy life. We are called to be light in the darkness.[14] We need to know what we treasure most. More importantly, we need to understand how to carry that, long-term.

The upside-down Kingdom of God isn't based on performance, rules and religion. It is brought to earth by sons and daughters. God our Father – 'Abba', as Jesus called Him – expects us to be 'shrewd as snakes and as innocent as doves' – for He is sending us out 'like sheep among wolves'.[15] Yet, He needs us to be childlike to become

---

13  See John 15:19.

14  1 Thessalonians 5:5

15  Matthew 10:16.

mature; extravagant yet self-controlled; letting go to take hold; stopping to move forward; risking to love; resting to work; powerful in extravagance; weak in being strong.

Before you move on, just take some time to allow what I have written to sink in. Begin to ask Jesus what you value most. Ask the Holy Spirit to show you and do some journaling with Him. Then commit to learning how to let go, to take hold.

Fix your eyes on Him. Take time to gaze, to look, to think, as
He meets you where you are.

# WEEK ONE

## Focus

**POSSIBILITY**

**PURPOSE**

**POTENTIAL**

**PROVISION**

# Possibility

There is a light shining in the darkness and it is greater than the darkness because when it shines the darkness is no longer dark.

The woman at the feet of Jesus, risking all she had by breaking the perfume and pouring it over His feet and head, reveals possibility at an extreme. Her extravagance drew from Jesus a response that proclaimed her message beyond her time into infinity, to all people. She did not hold back, she gave all she had, and she knew the most important treasure in her life. She had been given hope, 'the confident expectation that good is coming',[16] and she was celebrating.

---

16  Steve Backlund, Bethel Church, Redding, California (See Resources for his website)

Her intentional passion, reserved for the right time, the right place and the right person, speaks of the possibility of our doing the same to release and prepare those for whom we are placed in the world.

This prophetic act came out of love. The extravagance was criticised by religious-minded disciples who could not distinguish extravagance from waste, and had no spiritual eyes to see the truth. She had no concern as she knew who she was, what she had been rescued from, and who Jesus was to her. Nothing was more significant in her life than Him, which made her significant in history.

She had had to make decisions, choices that mattered. She had laid down her life to pick up the very gift that gave her life, and opened the possibility – gave hope – for disciples down through the ages to do the same, to see the same, and to love the same. Freedom brought her this sense of the possible, it gave her hope, because her treasure was the freedom-bringer – Freedom Himself. She was ready, in this instance, to take this opportunity to give Him everything. Her heart was prepared.

She is taking us back to our first ministry of intimacy and worship of Him. The place where nothing else matters and it seems the greatest gift to us is to break everything at Jesus feet. This is the place of our greatest worldly treasures being replaced by the greatest treasure of intimacy and living our lives in Jesus and the Father by the Holy Spirit.

It is out of this place that possibility emerges, where God says that, with Him, all things are possible.[17] It is a place of extravagant grace. We don't know whether the two stories in the Bible are about the same woman.[18] One is a woman who washes Jesus' feet with her tears, wipes them with her hair, and pours the perfume onto them, while He is reclining at the table. Instead of disapproving or finding Himself in discomfort, Jesus accepts that act and affirms her publicly. She is totally forgiven and therefore there is no record of her sin. Her gratitude is immense. The other woman anoints His head with oil. Are they the same woman, or different ones? The answer is the same: Jesus is where hope begins.

The woman was open to deep character change because of her passion for Jesus who became her whole life. She did not follow rules and regulations to accomplish her purpose, she followed her heart. She did not follow the many rules of the Pharisees, to prompt Jesus to tell the disciples that she would be remembered forever for her passion. She simply fell in love. She was grateful. She had been rescued. She was not perfect before she did this. We are told we will never be perfect, until we reach heaven. But she did allow Him to influence her heart and her actions.

This history-maker was receptive, open, willing, grateful, loving, generous and self-controlled. She did

---

17    See Matthew 19:26; Mark 10:27; Ephesians 3:20.

18    Matthew 26:6-13; Mark 14:3-11; Luke 7:36-50.

not react to the disciples. She allowed Jesus to speak. Her joy and worship of Jesus moved heaven, so that her name was written in history. The prophetic declaration of what she did came before the Holy Spirit was poured out. Jesus declared that she had done this to prepare Him for burial. She had a listening and obedient heart. She was a risk-taker. She did not mind being falsely accused, nor laughed at. She was prepared to do the extraordinary simply because He was Jesus.

She had learned that to overcome those who would take her gift and those who would undermine what was treasure to her, she would have to keep her focus on her treasure and know who she was. Her sense of identity with Jesus was paramount. Her royal call to release fragrance over Him was the 'one thing' for her. This 'one thing' defeated all the power that the enemy could throw at her and became the seal of her history-making.

## Practical steps

At this point in the book, we look at that first thoracic vertebra that connects this part of the spine to the neck, or the cervical spine. From it, we can turn our head to look in a different direction, and see possibility. We can look upwards to see the wonder of the skies and the expanse that is unending, lifting our face for the touch of the Holy Spirit. We can look downwards to our feet, to observe the new steps that we will be making. We can look forwards.

But never, can we look fully backwards from that vertebra. The past remains the past, and we are presented with possibility in the present, hope for the future.

May I advise you to find people, who do not live their lives in fear. Those who know God as a good Father and can walk with you. The ones who have been through their own journeys, and express this in their individual style.[19] If you do not know people around you like this, then ask the Father to bring you some. In the meantime, seek out some of the Resources I have put at the end of this book. They have helped us grow and mature over the past five years, and continue to do so. Look for 'fathers', and 'mothers', who truly know the meaning of this.

Get alone with God this week as many times as you can.

In my own healing journey, I found that faulty beliefs, fear, the influence of religion and performance that had surrounded me all my life and developed in my lifestyle, affected my physical posture so much that I was out of alignment. The fear of what people think about us, the religious constraints others expect us to live by, the belief that God is just waiting to punish – yet our Father draws near – when instilled deeply, flow out and infect every part of us and others. These beliefs drive us to achieve,

19   Galatians 5:1: 'It is for freedom that Christ has set us free. Stand firm, then, and do not let yourselves be burdened again by a yoke of slavery.'

to ignore the Father who says 'Come to Me, all you who are weary and burdened, and I will give you rest',[20] they set God up as a Taskmaster in a prison, giving orders and harshly punishing those who do not obey. These beliefs remove our true identity.

By the time I saw the physiotherapist, the problem was not simply muscle-based, but deep in the joints, and this had moved bones. I was physically fit, in dance ministry in my church – I had a deep relationship with God – but I was missing a large piece of the jigsaw of who God really is as a Father. Many of us are. So, breathing was difficult, fear was underlying continually and often overwhelming though I could not pinpoint it, and sitting, lying, walking or exercising were agonising.

In my journey of breaking out of these mindsets, I came to understand my Father in a deep way. As I began to go to the physiotherapist to loosen my joints, I had to commit a season to breaking every twenty minutes throughout the day, to stretch, to adjust and to refocus. That radical, life-saving discipline, in that season, became spiritual, helping me to make the time to take note of my thinking, what my body was feeling, and what my priorities were.

I developed five keys to bring me back on form. I will apply four of these at the end of days one to four, each week. Then I will use the fifth for days five and six, when there is no meditation so that you can reflect on what

20  See Matthew 11:28.

you have read on the first four days. The seventh day is a rest day. I call these keys, because they lead us through doors into spaces where we can open out our spirit, soul and body and receive from God. Through those doors, we experience a different world for a while.

If you are a mother with toddlers, then do what is possible. I used to take small instances at different points in the day, yet I rooted myself early in the morning, and set it as a priority because I found it gave me energy to care for them, particularly when my husband was away on dangerous military tours. It's all about finding what suits you best, and the book by Angela Ashwin, *Patterns Not Padlocks* (Eagle, 2000) may help you. I would say the same to men as I do to women. Set time. Meeting with God is not light and fluffy, it is tapping into the resurrection power of Jesus Christ, let alone developing your relationship! Too many men classify intimacy as a woman's arena. It is time to break out of that mould. It is where your power rests, your strength in weakness.

## THE POSTURE KEY:

- Sit on the edge of your chair with knees straight before you and feet flat on the ground. Physically draw your spine upwards. Reach your arms up and out, and push your shoulders down and back, whilst breathing in. Tilt your head back a little too. Feel the stretch in your thoracic spine. Hold for between fifteen and thirty seconds, breathing. Then relax and roll your shoulders up to your ears and backwards, a few times.

- Check the 'lordosis' in your lower back, that you have a curve forward there while you are sitting. Put a rolled-up towel behind your waist to help. Drop your shoulders down and a little back.

- Your chest, shoulders, back, and breathing will feel freer, your mind more refreshed and your eyes rested.

- Ask yourself the question, what do you currently think of God?

- Do you recognise any lies about His goodness?

## THE STOPPING KEY:

- Pause in what you are doing. Lift your face to God for a moment.
- Where do you require refocus now?
- What impossibility faces you?
- Do you know that God says, 'I'm Possible'?

## THE BREATHING KEY:

- Take some moments to breathe from your diaphragm, allowing your stomach to expand with the in-breath, and draw in with the out-breath. Breathe out longer than you breathe in.
- Focus on what it would look like if your 'impossibility' became 'possibility'.

## THE RELAXATION KEY:

- Simply close your eyes a moment.
- Let go of the Impossibility at Jesus' feet. Watch Him take it.
- Choose to believe that your Father God is good.

# Purpose

What you do on purpose, moves you into, or away from, God's purpose for your life.

Within the woman who poured out her treasure on Jesus in the Bible, her heart and her mind and her purpose changed. She had seen something in her heart that became a powerful and spiritual act that became an example for all of humanity. Jesus increased the treasure the woman poured from the broken alabaster vase, to become a purpose wider than she could imagine or see. You see, He had seen her heart.

She had one purpose in mind. To anoint Jesus' head and His feet. She used the one thing that she had, and received everything in return, because everything to her was to please Jesus and receive His love. Her purpose came out of what had already been done for her. Her purpose came out of her salvation, her redemption, her healing. Her purpose became clear when she was rescued.

She did what she did, on purpose, with intention, having planned. She would not have been there with an alabaster flask of perfume otherwise. Her doing on purpose moved her into God's purpose for her life. She was to be an example of extravagance forever. She was an Esther in her time, approaching the King, and becoming the decree to God's people of freedom, identity, authority and purpose.[21]

It is really very simple. Our purpose will always be a heart issue. Where is your heart?

You were created to live on purpose, with purpose. Even when we do not know fully what our personal purpose in life is, we know what God's purpose for humankind is. His purpose is that we would come to know Him, live in deep relationship with Him, and that the knowledge of His glory, which is His full character, would cover the earth as the waters cover the sea.[22] The woman fulfilled that. Jesus' character was shown not only in His response to her act of worship, but in what she did.

He wants to be intimate with us over and above anything that we are called to do. That intimacy will infuse us with His character so that streams of abundance flow out of us

---

21  Esther 4:14.

22  See Habakkuk 2:14; Isaiah 11:9.

over the world, creating a legacy of His goodness in the people who are brought to Him, forever down the ages.

This is astounding, that the Father God would want relationship, right now, with His created men and women so much that He sent His only Son, Jesus Christ, to earth to make the entire payment for our sin by dying on a cross after being beaten and insulted. Jesus was willing to do this for us. He knew His Father's love for Him, He always did what He saw His Father doing, and because of His great love for us He did it – love that sacrificed Himself so that we would not lose life. His purpose for us is freedom,[23] in deep intimacy with Himself, the Father and the Holy Spirit. That is indeed the most precious jewel to protect. Those with eyes to see will see.

This is our 'core strength'. Good posture all comes from our core, as posture is basically how we keep upright against gravity. By using our core strength, we avoid straining muscles that are doing work they were not created to do. That is why we exercise our core muscles. If therefore our core muscles in the spiritual world are our intimacy and relationship, then those are what we are to exercise most.

There is a perfect alignment for a healthy body towards which we aim, and this is also what we do spiritually. There are times when we need to learn to walk again,

---

23 Galatians 5:1 says: 'It is for freedom that Christ has set us free. Stand firm, then, and do not let yourselves be burdened again by a yoke of slavery.'

or sit properly, breathe and exercise well to readjust, or even for the first time. That has been my journey, and in the making of that journey and meditating on it, I have discovered deeper spiritual intimacy and relationship with the Lord. It is my story that I had to break out of discipline, to come into freedom and have discipline restored to me as the fruit of the Spirit of self-control. Harsh discipline is very different to self-control, and godly disciplines.

The woman with the perfume simply acted. She broke fear with the vase of love. 'Perfect love drives out fear'.[24] The fragrance filled the room and she had it on herself as well. She didn't fight. Jesus spoke for her, and her purpose was fulfilled.

## Practical steps

It is a spiritual and practical reality that when we begin anything we do out of the place of having been with God, ideas flow, and we are more able to see the purpose in what we are doing. We have simply invited the Holy Spirit to show us, and to fill us. At times, what we will be doing is only a small part of the whole and we will not always understand. The key is just to take that one step. The next will come. By being with God, I mean giving yourself

24   1 John 4:18 says 'There is no fear in love. But perfect love drives out fear, because fear has to do with punishment. The one who fears is not made perfect in love.'

a chance to connect with Him, and to invite Him in to everything – yet also setting aside specific times to meet with Him.

Commit time, maybe consider allocating this month to set aside for God to speak to you. Follow up on leads you feel you hear, about who to connect with, and dig into the Word. Make notes and discuss them with Him. This is a precious season. The journey takes time. You may find, as a mother or a father, that you hear God through your children some days! Being with God does not always mean solitary times labouring in prayer. Weave times into the day, into everything that you are doing. I used to do this while I cleaned the house, or walking to pick up the children from school. My husband uses times when he is on the treadmill, or out cycling.

I can't recommend highly enough, always carrying something to record with – and/or a piece of paper and pencil. Recording or making a note means that you do not have to try to remember what you had in your mind. It just frees you up. The less load in your mind, the better.

## THE POSTURE KEY:

- Stand up, and consciously sense the inward curve of your lower back, the outward curve of your upper back, and the gentle inward curve of your neck. Adjust your posture by sensing a cord from heaven that is connected to the top of your head, and let your shoulders drop downwards and a little backwards. Draw your spine upwards, aware of your core. Sometimes this must be a conscious, deliberate effort. So much loads us down and we become more tired with bad posture!

- Thank God for holding you upright. Ask the Holy Spirit to come.
- Ask Him to show you what is most valuable to you.
- Write it down.

## THE STOPPING KEY:

- Face up to the Father a moment, and sense His breath on your face.
- Tell Him you love Him! You may feel an immediate response. Be ready for that. If not today, then be open on other days! Begin to develop your senses to pick up His Spirit movements towards and around you.

## THE BREATHING KEY:

- Breathe from your diaphragm for a few minutes. Allow your stomach to expand with the in-breath, and draw in with the out-breath. Breathe out longer than you breathe in. This is an exercise we learn too in Emotional Intelligence,[25] to calm ourselves.
- Imagine God readjusting your priorities. Let Him do it. When you fail, as we all will, just do it again.

## THE RELAXATION KEY:

- Let the Father bring a peace to your heart, while you breathe out priorities that are not His, and let Him replace them when you breathe in. Let go and walk around a bit.

---

25 Travis Bradberry and Jean Greaves, *Emotional Intelligence 2.0.* (TalentSmart® 2009)

DAY
THREE

# Potential

*Our potential contains the explosive resurrection power that confounds religion, blows apart restriction, and raises people from the grave.*

I wanted to write there: 'Handle with care!' The word 'potential' has a root in the Latin *potentia*, meaning power, might, force, and *potens*, from which we derive the word 'potent'. In the context I am using it, potential is not simply possibility. I see it as a real and raw potency within, which if developed and allowed to mature will powerfully touch those around us and into the future. Possibility says potential will be released. God will do the work to bring us to that point, though we will co-labour with the Holy Spirit! That takes time.

It is interesting to note that the woman anointed Jesus beforehand for His burial, as He said, without any prior understanding that this would be the potential outcome of her act. She also had no knowledge beforehand that her act would be told over and over and that it would break through into history, shattering the religious spirit, demonstrating pure-hearted worship. Jesus said that 'the true worshippers will worship the Father in the Spirit and in truth, for they are the kind of worshippers the Father seeks'. [26]

She simply had no idea of the potential of what she was about to do before she did it. She knew only the facts: that the perfume was costly and rich and fragrant and that it would linger on Him, in the household, and on her. She knew that once she had done it, there was no going back for the vase was broken and the perfume poured. She knew too that it would be a personal act of devotion and worship, from her heart, and that she would need courage to do it.

God makes fruitful what is from the heart, whatever is by faith. Nothing done without faith is fruitful – striving religiously has no place in the Kingdom of heaven. Fruitful in His eyes is not necessarily fruitful in the world's eyes. He looks for those who worship Him in Spirit and in truth. What we are capable of may not be what He is looking for. Think about it.

The young boy who brought the loaves and fishes to Jesus, a small lunch that cost him a lot both in producing

26  John 4:23.

19

it, and the fact that without it he had nothing with which to feed himself, had no idea of the potential of his act. I am sure that his mouth dropped when he saw what Jesus produced from his offering! His offering had the potential to feed the 5,000, with leftovers, satisfying their hunger, when this boy brought the food to Jesus – yet, he did not know that. This had the power to bring life to those who had experienced the miracle. It was potent. A simple act was potent. The potential to feed that many people with leftovers was actualised through Jesus' faith and obedience.

Yet again this shows that the heart (intimacy, relationship) is the key posture principle. Where potential is concerned, our heart posture can move God's heart way beyond that horizon we see. In physics, the gravitational potential energy of an object can be worked out. In God, it seems that potential is not a fixed point – it is impossible to see or discover the end of His ability and therefore ours! He is the God of increase, according to the heart.

It is helpful to note that when God gives us a prophecy about our potential – and I talk about prophecy later in this book – though we see it as immediately available, there is usually a process to activate before we reach that potential. This is because we have heart-bugs – little things that have grown to block our intimacy with Him and our understanding of our identity. He kindly places a 'joy' before us to help us to journey towards that, and deal with the blockages on the way. When we live with the knowledge that God has made us to accomplish things much greater than we can see, then we find the courage to deal with the heart-bugs on the way. God in His goodness, as a Father, will only show us what is necessary at the time, and what He gives us the strength to deal with through His own Holy Spirit.

Imagine owning a garden shed full of wonderful gardening equipment, brand new and shiny, but not being able to open the shed, because you have no key. It is locked, because the equipment needs protecting: both from thieves, and from young children who do not know how to use it and for whom it would be dangerous to use. To own the key, you would either need to be the owner of the shed, or a skilled gardener employed to care for the owner's garden. On the other hand, you may have lost the key, being paranoid and having hidden it so well that you can no longer find it, in which case a lock change would be required.

Either way, you know the equipment is there. Who you are and whether you understand who you are, will be the determining factor as to whether you will be able to access the brand-new, shiny garden equipment. Just as allowing a child to have the key would be dangerous, and you would care for that child and protect it from accessing this potential until he or she was mature enough to use it well, so allowing us to use our full potential without the process of maturity would be foolish. At the same time that potential needs to be kept safe inside us, cared for and held ready, by fighting with the prophecies given to us. Spiritual thieves in the form of lies and random 'opportunities' will use unofficial keys. That door needs a good God-lock on it so that when the time to use His key comes, we are ready. We need to have ears to hear what our Father is saying.

## Practical steps

As we reach our third day of the first week, it is time to go for a walk; try to take at least ten minutes, but if more is possible, walk for more than thirty minutes. These walking times are great building blocks, as we can chat with God the Father, Jesus, and the Holy Spirit about anything and everything. Remember, taking a recorder with you, or your mobile phone and knowing how to record, is very useful. I record any important thoughts I want to follow up, any decisions, anything God might have said to me, and then I listen back at home and write down anything that I want to keep, whilst deleting the rest. It is a way of developing your thinking ability, creative stream, and your relationship with God.

Rather like Adam and Eve walked in the garden with God, it is wonderful to do this in the morning first thing, or in the evening, when our day is finished. Any time is possible, though.

Use this time to reflect on things that you have read this week.

## THE POSTURE KEY:

- When you have finished walking, stretch your arms upwards, and then lower them back by your sides. Then slowly bend your body forwards, starting with your head and moving down your spine, until you are hanging down with your hands reaching for the ground, soft knees, feet flat, and shoulder-width apart. Hang like that for a count of thirty. Then slowly unbend your back, working upwards from the base of your spine, ending with your neck straightening, until you are upright again.

- If you cannot, and cannot reach further than halfway, do not worry! You will be able to, the more you do this. Please remember that if you have medical problems that hinder movement, make sure you check with your doctor. However, this is a common stretch.

## THE STOPPING KEY:

- Pause before you go back inside. Thank the Father for something in your life. Continue if you want to!

## THE BREATHING KEY:

- Spend some moments breathing as we have been learning, from your diaphragm. While you do, ask the Holy Spirit to highlight anything in your life He wants to speak to you about.

## THE RELAXATION KEY:

- Lie on your back on the floor inside. Continue your breathing. Let your muscles relax after your walk. Use the following verses:

Psalm 139:23-24:

Search me, God, and know my heart; test me and know my anxious thoughts. See if there is any offensive way in me, and lead me in the way everlasting.

NOTE: If you do hear anything from the Holy Spirit that you need to look at with Him, then simply write it down, talk to Him about it, let out your feelings if you need to, and begin to think about what the way forward is. If you need healing then check the back of this book for places you can find that.

- However, often it could be very simple to deal with – confessed, repented of, and forgiven, immediately. Then it does not blot your record anymore! Fabulous. Keep short accounts with God.

- Remember, God does not accuse, the devil does. Jesus is your Advocate. God is your Father. You are His child. He will only deal with things at a suitable time, one by one. He does not overwhelm you with guilt nor with shame. Focus on the 'joy of your salvation'.[27] Jesus died for you. Stand firm against lies. You are amazing, loved and treasured, with great hope.

---

27  Psalm 51:12.

DAY
FOUR

# Provision

Open wide your mouth and I will fill it.
*Psalm 81:10b*

Our perception of our needs changes according to where our focus is fixed. The woman with the alabaster vase of perfume in the Bible had a completely different viewpoint to the disciples there, as to what was valuable. She also had an expanded vision of how to value what was valuable in her life.

Judas complained when she broke the vase and poured the rich perfume over Jesus' feet and on his head. It challenged his narrow principles, shook his understanding of Jesus' heart, and allowed the disciples to see a God they had never seen before.

Their understanding was, that the money could be given to the poor if the flask of perfume had been sold. The woman's understanding was that she had been forgiven much, received much from Jesus and He deserved everything that she had. She trusted for provision, having poured out her provision upon Him. Her way had to depend on faith.[28]

She received criticism for her action. Jesus, however, showed great joy over her act. She herself provided for the disciples a glimpse of a Jesus they had never seen, nor understood, before.

To the end of her life, and into eternity, she could hold the knowledge that He was pleased with her, and it was He who shouted her fame beyond her day, beyond her region.

What is our perspective on provision? As we change, we will find ourselves making choices that surprise us, about our lifestyle, to fit our new focus. A discipline of looking to God for His input each day gives Him opportunity to speak into our hearts and put words in our mouths. An attitude of trust will grow, that a loving Father will give us what we need.[29] An openness to the Holy Spirit to guide our feet in the right paths[30] that day will develop as we spend intimate time with God each day. As we read the Word, our hearts

---

28   See Hebrews 11:1, NKJV; Romans 1:17, NKJV.

29   See Psalm 23:1.

30   See Psalm 23:3.

and minds are washed with it so that renewal becomes reality as we walk out in our daily lives what it says.[31]

Just as developing a real relationship takes time and effort, so we grow a dependence on a loving Father. Our ability to 'ask' and trust that it will be given us[32] will increase as we experience His answers, and as we understand what it is that is on His heart for which we need to ask. The heart of a true Father wants to give us what is good for us and loves His children to come to Him and ask Him for it.

Experience of God in life, knowing ourselves as a deeply loved son or daughter to whom the Father gives all good things without measure, and with pleasure, is the key to receiving.

Knowing God as good, always and forever protects us in the times when things do not go the way we expected. Reminding ourselves of the times when He came through for us and for others, noting these down when they happen so that we can draw them out like a sword in the difficult moments, all protect the jewel that we are running with. The interesting point about provision is that it is not always what you expect. If we take Paul's example, he told us that he could be content whatever situation he found himself in.[33] This meant that even when he was in lack,

31  See James 1:22-25.

32  See Matthew 7:7.

33  See Philippians 4:11

he trusted God and found Him faithful – God had been faithful to him before, so he knew He could be trusted in any new situation.

For Paul, to live was Christ.[34] Jesus was Paul's 'one thing'. He was the reason for everything and the only One he desired. His relationship with God meant that God simply provided everything that Paul needed to live and do the work he was given to do. This did not mean no hardship, neither did it mean no hard work. But it did mean total dependence. If you are like me, that kind of attitude takes a while to develop and it needs selecting reverse gear when we find ourselves running down a false track! Our perspective on provision changes as we experience more of God.

Paul was clear that he had not yet reached perfection.[35] Perfectionists fail before they have begun. Those who position themselves to run the race, seeing the prize, yet knowing they have not yet obtained it can fall, but still pick themselves back up and keep on running. They look at what they have tripped over and learn, and move on.

That is our posture. The provision of our Father's lap, where we can retreat and hear His voice, know that we are His children and not expected to be perfect, gives us the will to know our Father who is perfect. When we

34   See Philippians 1:21
35   Philippians 3:12,14

lean on His chest and receive new strength and guidance we can get back up, climb down from His lap and run again.

## Practical steps

Every day, begin by thanking God for each piece of armour He gives us, ensuring that we are wearing it and have not climbed out of it overnight! Go to Ephesians 6:10-18 and think about these verses awhile. Then make a list of the armour, and begin to reflect on it every morning. This will build your awareness and understanding of it. For instance, realise that the truth sets you free – see John 8:31-32! You have truth, Jesus' teaching that sets you free, buckled around your core! Ask the Holy Spirit to fill you and keep you filled throughout that day. Tell Him anything with which you could do with His help. You co-labour with God, so He will be all too happy to hear! Let Him have your anxiety about it and wait a moment to feel Him take it. Sometimes I walk about the garden in the summer, in the early morning, doing this.

### THE POSTURE KEY:

Today, do this simple stretching exercise three times. It will loosen the muscles in your upper back, leaving them more flexible and therefore more comfortable in your work during the day:

- Sit upright on a chair, feet flat on the floor. Cross your arms over your chest like an X. Twist from your waist first to the left, hold briefly, then to the right, hold again. Repeat ten times each side. Keep your head as it would normally be in relation to your chest, don't twist your head round. Make sure your hips remain pointing forwards.

## THE STOPPING KEY:

- At three points today, stop whatever you are doing and close your eyes, and turn your face up to Jesus. Thank Him for His blessing and smile!

## THE BREATHING KEY:

- Spend some moments breathing as we have been learning, from your diaphragm.
- Whilst you do this, bring to mind those things that you feel you need. On your outward breath, release them to God, knowing that He has heard your prayer.

## THE RELAXATION KEY:

- Break off at some point in the day, get out a sketch pad or any kind of paper. Find some colour pens, pencils, or paints. Use five to thirty minutes, to draw, colour, paint. If you do not consider yourself an artist, just doodle and see what happens. Have some worship music on if you wish. Simply let your mind run, and let go. It is worth asking the Holy Spirit to come and touch you and your time, because often you will find that what you have drawn or doodled will be something that impacts you. Sometimes, it will just be fun messing around.

DAY FIVE

# The Soaking Key

Try to set aside ten to thirty minutes, in which you get comfortable, close your eyes, and do nothing except allow yourself to sink deep into God's love. Put on suitable music and let it happen. It can be useful to keep your notebook journal beside you and write down what you might hear in that time. Let Him encourage your heart and plant seeds of hope. Lying on a beanbag, on cushions on the floor, sitting in an armchair, or on the floor with your back against the wall, all work well.

# The Soaking Key

Do the same as yesterday, and set aside ten to thirty minutes, in which you get comfortable, close your eyes, and do nothing except allow yourself to sink deep into God's love. Put on suitable music if you want. Remember to keep your notebook journal beside you and write down what you might hear in that time. Let Him encourage your heart and plant seeds of hope.

This week we have particularly focused on hope, and we have talked about beliefs.[36]

---

36 If you need further help, why not visit www.ignitinghope.com, full of resources to encourage you? See also the Resources listed at the back of this book.

These are the vertebrae, the principles, we have looked at this week:

Possibility

Purpose

Potential

Provision

They have developed our Focus.

## Prayer:

Father, we come to You as Your precious sons and daughters, deeply loved. We ask for Your supernatural increase to touch the keys we are using, to open our hearts more to Your passion for us. We fix our eyes on Jesus and are amazed at the abundant life He opened up for us through His cross. We thank You, Holy Spirit, that You are our Guide, and that we do not run alone.

Now, prepare to spend Day Seven with rest in our hearts.

Know the depths of the grace of the Lord Jesus, the heights of the love of the Father, and the width of the wisdom from the Holy Spirit, in your life!

# WEEK TWO

# ESTABLISHING

**PROTECTION**

**PREPARATION**

**PROMISE**

**PROPHECY**

# Protection

The abiding principle remains abiding.

The woman anointing Jesus was not protected from the disciples' comments and disdain. She just didn't count them worthy of attention. Her attention was fixed on Jesus. It was His voice that sent a shiver through the disciples of gentle rebuff, and His voice that affirmed, and anointed her with His blessing.

To be fully protected, we need to know our enemy, and we need to recognise God's voice above the devil's. In any battle, if we do not know our enemy, his strategy and tactics, we have lost. In worldly battles, we are expected to fight. In the Kingdom of God, Jesus fought and won for us. We live and fight from His victory. Our fight, our struggle, is not against flesh and blood[37] but against spiritual forces, and we need a spiritual response. Our fight is against the lies that the devil sends into our minds, to shift us from the ground already won in Jesus, to fight a battle that is not ours to fight. He wants to dislodge us so we fall into striving for something already won. Our strategy is to stand, and continue to stand, in what we know of God and what Jesus has done on the cross for us. We push back the lies with our shield of faith, we cut them away with our sword of the Spirit, we head-butt, deflect, the enemy's lies with the salvation we recognise, that is our helmet over our minds.

The very jewel that we are protecting – an intimate, open relationship with our God – is our protection. The struggle itself to keep focus, to capture our thoughts, to remain in the place of abiding, to let go, and to let God love us, is our battle. If our thoughts are busy and negative, that is our striving: we need to take them captive to Jesus[38] and replace those thoughts with noble, positive, worthwhile thoughts. When we are so wrapped up in Him that we set knowing Him above our trials, our heart can be inaccessible to the enemy forces. Yet while we remain on this earth, persistence will always be necessary.

Has anyone noticed that when we are thinking negative thoughts and feeling oppressed, negative things

37  Ephesians 6:12.

38  See 2 Corinthians 10:5.

happen more frequently? Our thoughts carry emotions attached, which form attitudes. Our attitudes cannot be hidden and they affect other people around us. Attitudes lead to actions, which increase the negativity around our lives.[39]

The devil comes only to steal and kill and destroy.[40] He has one purpose in mind, to separate us from God. Without God, we are nothing and we are easily toppled. So, the enemy knows full well that intimacy is the greatest weapon against him that we have. He knows that if he drowns out God's gentle whisper with bombardments of loud lies in our heads – which he is perfectly capable of planting – then we will live unprotected and drifting backwards and forwards.[41] The promise of God that He will never leave us nor forsake us[42] sends shivers through the enemy camp – especially as He repeats it several times.

The woman did not point out the disciples and tell Jesus to protect her and rebuke them. She simply loved Him, and worshipped Him. She seemed oblivious of them. He acted because of that. She did not have to fight for her place, for her reputation, nor for her validation. He put that seal upon her. It was His name, His glory and

39   See Dr Caroline Leaf, *Switch On Your Brain*, for more on this (See Resources)

40   John 10:10.

41   See James 1:5-8.

42   See Joshua 1:5; Hebrews 13:5; Deuteronomy 31:8; Deuteronomy 31:6; and John 14:18 says, 'I will not leave you as orphans; I will come to you.'

His fame she carried from then on. She had the mark of authority in intimacy.

So how can we establish that in our own lives? We have many alabaster jars to break. We have the jar of Time; of Reputation; of Riches; of Ego, anything that comes as a hindrance to our relationship with Jesus. Establishing rest in our lives, by knowing our 'one thing', was never going to be easy, unless we have really decided in our minds what our 'one thing' is. Then, we will be able to say 'No' to that which is not our 'one thing'. Kris Vallotton[43] of Bethel Church, California, points out that if you have a big enough 'Yes', your 'No' will be easy.

Jesus told us that while we are in the world we will have trouble.[44] We are not part of the world and so we will always live with tension unless we know who we are, who God is to us, and why we are here. Our Kingdom is of another world.

Romans 7 speaks of the battle that we wage when we do not know who we are and where we are from. Many people think that is a normal battle. But it is not! Romans 8 speaks of overcoming through knowing our identity, receiving our new DNA, our new life, and leaving our old selves dead in the grave. Our old self died. We do not have to fight it!

---

43  Kris Vallotton, senior associate leader of Bethel Church, Redding, California and co-founder of Bethel School of Ministry.

44  See John 16:33.

Paul had hardships. Jesus died on a cross. Yet in them all we can know that our Father protects. Stephen died whilst being stoned, looking up into heaven where he was shown the glory of God, and Jesus standing at the right hand of God.[45] Whilst being falsely accused before the Sanhedrin, his face was seen by them to have been like that of an angel.[46] He was protected within the most horrific death and in the midst of false witnesses. His identity in Christ was secure, his purpose understood, and his destiny assured.

He had won the battle for his mind[47] to such an extent that he could ignore not only the lies of the enemy in his head telling him to be afraid, but also the people around him who told him he was very wrong, and in great trouble. He was satisfied with Who he knew, and the big 'Yes' he had said. He even fell to his knees and forgave his persecutors throwing stones at him. Then, it says, he 'fell asleep'.[48] Wow. I think he knew the secret of abiding.

## Practical steps

I have found that it takes time to recognise lies, and that pinning Post-it notes to my mirror which I see morning and

---

45  Acts 7:55.

46  Acts 6:15.

47  Mark Iles, School for Prophecy, first teaching session of *Developing Your Prophetic Gift*, see Resources

48  Acts 7:60.

night, helps! I write down verses that have been highlighted to me about my identity in Christ, the Father who loves me, the Holy Spirit who enables me, and about my 'sonship'. I use declarations as well.[49] I make lists on my Twitter account of a few trusted people who are authentic and encouraging, and take some time to review what they are tweeting.

More recently, I have also worked through Dr Caroline Leaf's book, *Switch On Your Brain*, which I will be using for a while yet!

Most importantly, and above all of these things, has been having spiritual fathers and mothers in my life who tell me who I am. Who tell me when I am not being who I am. Who love me whatever I am like. I cannot stress the importance of that enough.

## THE POSTURE KEY:

- As last week, sit on the edge of your chair with knees straight before you and feet flat on the ground. Physically draw your spine upwards. Reach your arms up and out, and push your shoulders down and back, whilst breathing in. Tilt your head back a little too. Feel the stretch in your thoracic spine. Hold for between fifteen and thirty seconds,

---

49 See Steve and Wendy Backlund's teaching on their website listed in Resources.

breathing. Then relax and roll your shoulders up to your ears and backwards a few times.

- Check the 'lordosis' in your lower back, that you have a curve forward there while you are sitting. Put a rolled up towel behind your waist to help. Drop your shoulders down and a little back.

- Your chest, shoulders and back, and breathing will feel freer, your mind more refreshed and your eyes rested.

Ask yourself the question:

Do you recognise any lies telling you that you are not a child of God?

Then you know where they are coming from! If you have committed your life to Jesus Christ then you are a child of God and you have a new DNA. If you have not, then the invitation is there.

## THE STOPPING KEY:

- Pause, lift your face to God for a moment, worship Him and feel His warmth come upon you. Yes, God uses our senses, He created them. We will not always feel something, but to believe that we will, helps.

- Where do you need to renew your thinking?
- Take a little time and read Paul's letter to the Galatians over this month. Try a version like *The Message*, or *The Passion Translation*, to get you thinking differently.

## THE BREATHING KEY:

- Take some moments to breathe from your diaphragm, allowing your stomach to expand with the in-breath, and draw in with the out-breath. Breathe out longer than you breathe in.

## THE RELAXATION KEY:

- Put some music on, and get up and dance! It doesn't have to be long – but often it shifts mood, lifts our hearts in praise and gets the blood flowing! Dance because you are free, you are safe in Christ Jesus. By dance, I mean: move!

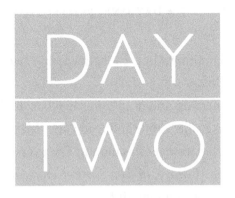

# Preparation

Preparation is an adventure that brings us ever closer
to God

Just as the perfume was prepared for its purpose from
costly oils, carefully mixed and balanced to give the valuable fragrance, so we are prepared for the specific role in
life for which we have been created.

Banning Liebscher recently said, 'Anytime God intends
to move, he first calls people to separate themselves for
His cause'.[50] Preparation time is needed. In the woman
with the alabaster vase, a change was required that altered
the purpose for the costly perfume. 'Her heart and her
mind, and her purpose changed, and it was something

---

50   Banning Liebscher, European Leaders' Advance Harrogate, 2017.

that she saw in her heart then became a really powerful and spiritual act.'[51]

It takes time for God to move our hearts and remove the trappings of the world and our past. The journey is one that takes us deeper into Him, where He can convince us of His love, which enables us to let go. It is a beautifying, a healing, a shift that moves us into His purposes. He creates in us a singleness of heart that begins to understand, over time, what is truly important to us. Without this, we have no big 'Yes'.[52]

Esther did not become Queen without preparation.[53] Twelve months were set apart for beautification. For her particular journey, she also needed to be spiritually prepared. Her heart was obedient and she took instruction. She was teachable, and open. When we read about her journey of preparation, we see that six months of it was with oil of myrrh, before she even reached six months with perfumes and preparations for beautifying women. Myrrh is described in Song of Songs 4:14, in The Passion Translation notes, as follows: 'Known as "tears from a tree", myrrh was a resin spice formed by cutting a tree. It is a picture of the suffering love of Christ dripping down from Calvary's tree.' How interesting, that it is Esther 4:14

---

51   Mark Iles, prophecy to me 18 March 2014.

52   Kris Vallotton teaches on the importance of a big 'Yes' in our lives, which means 'No' comes easily.

53   See Esther chapter 2:1-18

that speaks of Esther's call to count the cost of speaking, for such a time, for the freedom of her people.

Yet let's not forget the second six months! As *we* are prepared, God pours out on us, by the Holy Spirit, the precious 'oil of joy instead of mourning', He gives us 'a garment of praise instead of a spirit of despair'.[54]

Our preparation must include a deep revelation of Christ's sacrifice for us on the cross. Not only that, it includes acknowledgment that though the joy of knowing Him and being loved by Him is above all things, we will also experience suffering in our lives if we follow Him.[55] However, Paul says that his suffering was nothing compared to knowing Christ![56] And of Jesus, in the letter to the Hebrews, Paul says: 'For the *joy* that was set before him he endured the cross, scorning its shame, and sat down at the right hand of the throne of God.'[57] How does that fit together?

Esther was told by Mordecai, her cousin and the one who brought her up, in 4:14: 'For if you remain silent at this time, relief and deliverance for the Jews will arise from another place, but you and your father's family will perish. And who knows but that you have come to your royal position for such a time as this?'

---

54   Isaiah 61:3.

55   See 2 Timothy 3:12.

56   See Philippians 3:7-11.

57   Hebrews 12:2, my italics.

She had been called to her position by God for a purpose that was beyond just herself. She was called to deliver a whole nation. Her response came out of her preparation. She sent a message to her cousin requesting that he gather all the Jews in that city to fast for her, and she and her maids would do likewise, neither eating nor drinking for three days. At the end of that, she told him, she would go to the king, which was against the law. Her words were: 'And if I perish, I perish' (4:16)!

How ready are we to face the journey? How teachable? The journey could take many years. God knows how long He needs to beautify you. Yet the journey is wonderful! It means we can get to know Him, to spend time with Him, to learn from Him and to be His big kid. We can laugh and worship and enjoy His presence. The journey is about intimacy and coming to know Him. It is about coming to know ourselves, because maturity is self-awareness.

It is wonderful, too, because in coming to know ourselves we are ready to accept that we cannot do it ourselves. We can finally be real. We will never be perfect in this life, and that is the beauty of it. None of us are. Jesus did it all for us. The common denominator for our journeys is that it is only by grace we have been saved, through faith, not by works.[58] So, everything we do is nothing compared with what He has done for us already.

58   Ephesians 2:8-9.

That's extravagance: the more we understand that all our preparation was done already by Jesus on the cross, the more we will understand that there is no depth we can go to where He is not. The extravagance of grace. The place where He prepares us, where we are forgiven and eternally accepted and allowed to fail, where we are picked up again, dusted off, and set back on our feet.

There is no depth of preparation we can visit where He is not waiting with the gift of our life that He bought. There is nothing we can see about ourselves anymore that can shock us enough to stop our journey, and the more we know who we would be without Him, the more prepared we are. Knowing ourselves. This is the journey of beautification, of sanctification, yet it is also the journey of deep joy because we are already saved, set free and delivered, whole in Christ.

## Practical steps

Preparation is a beautiful 'vertebra', coming as it does halfway down the thoracic spine. Central to preparation is our meeting with God because it is in the secret place of the heart that He prepares us. It is often in the unseen places that preparation happens. God is in those places, and He sees. Practise, this week, being aware of God around your home, around your workplace, and consider what He is seeing. Feel His pleasure when you are being who He created you to be, and when you choose to listen to Him or be in His presence.

Those costly ointments that Esther was prepared with before she became Queen, are what we can imagine as we spend this time before the Lord. Imagination is a precious gift from God, one that we are to use.

## THE POSTURE KEY:

- Stand up, and consciously sense the inward curve of your lower back, the outward curve of your upper back, and the gentle inward curve of your neck. Adjust your posture by sensing a cord from heaven that is connected to the top of your head, and let your shoulders drop downwards and a little backwards. Draw your spine upwards, aware of your core.

- Thank God for holding you upright. Ask the Holy Spirit to come.

- Ask Him to show you the oil of joy and let it come into you.

## THE STOPPING KEY:

- Face up to the Father a moment, and sense His breath on your face.

- Thank Him for the preparation that is to come, and the blessing of knowing Him.

## THE BREATHING KEY:

- Breathe from your diaphragm for a few minutes. Allow your stomach to expand with the in-breath, and draw in with the out-breath. Breathe out longer than you breathe in.

  This is a good exercise to do when you are meditating too. Take a verse and breathe as you think about it.

## THE RELAXATION KEY:

Sit in a comfortable seat with a cup of coffee or tea (or a hot drink that you enjoy), and imagine Jesus sitting with you while you meditate on Isaiah 61:1-3. Hear Him speak those verses out and prepare your heart to receive them.

# Promise

He will keep you steady and strong to the very end,
making your character mature so that you will be found
innocent on the day of our Lord Jesus Christ. God is
forever faithful and can be trusted to do this in you, for
he has invited you to co-share the life of his Son, Jesus,
the Anointed One, our King!

*1 Corinthians 1:8,9 TPT*

The truth is that Jesus has given us a promise that He is
going to finish the work He has begun in us. It is His work,
and His alone. He promised the woman who poured out
all she was, all she had, upon Him, that what she had done
would be proclaimed wherever the gospel was preached,
forever. Simply because she loved. He has been true to His
Word, and He still is. The greatest promise is that Jesus
will never stop loving us. Everything is about love.

Think about it for a minute. This love must mean that we are loved whatever we have done, whatever point of our journey we have reached – because none of us are perfect, and we all make mistakes. That is part of maturing, and recognising who we are.

God's love is *agape* love. This kind is unconditional, and is not the normal love we talk about in the world, the one based upon performance, or the selfish love, nor the romantic love.

We have His promise, remember, that He will never leave us nor forsake us.[59] That means, even in our darkest, deepest pits. There is never a place we cannot have His joy, His presence, because in that place, He is.[60] He promises us the safest, most secure, relationship we can ever experience. And it is in, and out from, that place that we need to posture ourselves to receive everything in life and give anything, to anybody.

The promise is not all about achievement. It is not about performance accomplishing what He has promised. It is simply about loving Him, being loved by Him, and about being His.

If we read Song of Songs, we will see that there is a progression of relationship, just as there is when a bride is wooed. The depth gets deeper. The passion becomes

---

59  Joshua 1:5; Deuteronomy 31:8; Deuteronomy 31:6; Hebrews 13:5; Psalm 9:10.

60  See Psalm 139:7-12.

stronger. It is the same when Jesus is wooing the Bride, and the Bride is being prepared: His Bride, His Church, is made ready in Revelation. It has been a process, yes, but there is a promise to it. *He will* finish what He has begun in His Church. He is interested in each individual person in His Bride – each bride – each of us. A marriage is not based on performance or achievement, it is based upon unconditional love, persistence, long-term promise and covenant, through thick and thin.

That also applies to those promises that He has personally given to us, to our families, to our church, to our cities, or our nations and the world. There is a huge place in our prayer lives where we can remind God our Father that He has promised to give us what we ask when it is in line with His will.

Bringing us into the profoundly simple and practical, we could say it is like coming to a good Father and saying, 'Daddy! You said you'd take me to the playpark today! Can we go? Can we go?' whilst running to get our boots because we know the answer will be yes. We have a Daddy who sweeps us up, gives us a tight squeeze; then puts on His rain jacket, opens the door, takes our hand and runs with us. We both get muddy. We share our life. He does what He promised.

It's a relationship. It is time to listen to what God is doing, and wants to do with us, to write down what we hear, to follow up and ask for those things, talking to God about them and standing on the answers to those things He has promised. Then, go and get our boots on.

The Bible is full of promises that we can remind Him of, and receive in our lives. Make it fun, enjoy doing this with Him. There are also those direct words He has planted in our souls through dreams, listening and other people.

We remind ourselves – we *re-mind* ourselves – when we do this. The more we pray and speak out His promises, the more our own mind is remade.

Promise is defined as telling someone that you will certainly do something. God's faithfulness never lets us down. We can be confident that He does what He says He will do. When He speaks, it is a promise.

This kind of speaking into being is what we as prophetic people need to aim towards. Everything God says is Yes and Amen.[61] When we speak, our words need to be sharpened arrows, hitting the mark. When we fail, we know grace over our lives. We learn from mistakes and try again. Yet God's Word is promise and it never fails. He is different from us. Speak life into the dry bones.

## Practical steps

It is the third day of the second week, and it is time again for a walk. I suggest taking time every day to do some kind of exercise. The body was made for movement. So

---

61 See 2 Corinthians 1:20.

was our soul, and our spirit – we become freer, fresher and functioning in all three areas! Blood flow improves heart and lung function, as well as helping healing. It also clears the mind, and helps us to think. We become more positive through the release of endorphins. Daylight is important both for Vitamin D, and for this increase in inner good feeling.

Try to take at least ten minutes, but if more is possible, walk for more than thirty minutes – after work, or before work, sometime in the day if you work from home or, as I did, straight after you drop the children at school. Escape somewhere beautiful for an hour or forty-five minutes occasionally. Treasure it. Go whatever the weather – use waterproofs if you must! When you return, you will sleep better at night, and you will work better during the rest of the day.

These times that I remember taking during school drop days were key to my future. They were times that I could just let go to God and hear from Him. He gave me promises, and showed me things. At the same time I kept fit so I was able to do my work and manage the household while my husband was away.

Often, these times were hard to fit in – they had to be made a priority. For eighteen months, for instance, my drive to school and back, each end of the day, would be three hours in total to keep continuity at the same school during a house-move we had had to make. For the rest of the day I would be working hard at home, and in the evening, on my own while my husband was on dangerous military tours, I would be helping the children, and going out to serve in my church or running groups. No, it is not easy, I understand. But it is worth it.

So many of the promises I heard during those walks have come to fruition. Be encouraged.

## THE POSTURE KEY:

- Once again, when you have finished walking, stretch your arms upwards, and then put them back by your sides. Then slowly bend your body forwards until you are hanging down with your hands reaching for the ground, soft knees, feet flat, and shoulder-width apart. Hang like that for a count of thirty. Then slowly unbend your back, working upwards from the base of your spine, ending with your neck straightening, until you are upright again.
- There are many stretches one can do after exercise – look them up on the internet. It has become a discipline for me, as otherwise I spend the day with tight muscles.

## THE STOPPING KEY:

- Pause before you go back inside. Thank the Father for a promise that He has shown you.

## THE BREATHING KEY:

- Breathe as we have been learning, from your diaphragm.

## THE RELAXATION KEY:

- Take a moment over a cup of coffee or other beverage in the day, to consider a promise God has made you. Write it down, and pin it to your fridge or your mirror.

# Prophecy

Don't minimize the powerful gift that operates in your life, for it was imparted to you by the laying on of hands of the elders and was activated through the prophecy they spoke over you. Make all of this your constant meditation and make it real with your life so everyone can see that you are moving forward.

1 Timothy 4:14, TPT

The woman with the costly perfume had to be seeing with the eyes of her heart. There is no way we would break into our life-savings without seeing some important reason to do so, or have a depth of love beyond understanding for the one to whom we are giving it. She made a prophetic act by pouring the perfume upon Jesus. Prophecy uses the eyes of our heart, not the eyes of our head.[62] It requires acting on and in faith.

Words carry power. They can bring life, or death;[63] consider, for instance, the decree that King Ahasuerus allowed Haman to write and seal with the king's seal, that carried the death sentence on the nation of the Jews. There was no revoking the king's decree.[64] Yet Queen Esther risked her life twice by using her voice and influence. She found herself and her cousin Mordecai, who had trained her and brought her up, composing and sealing decrees to her nation who were Jews, that gave them power to fight back and claim life. It caused a breakout of rejoicing and feasting, and the fear of the Lord came upon the citizens who were not Jews, with conversions following. Freedom was announced and it broke the power of death.

Our words are to carry freedom, to break the old traditions, to give life to dry bones and to draw out what is precious in people. We were given grace by our Saviour, and therefore we are to pass that grace onwards. We are not there to condemn. The Holy Spirit does not condemn. Prophecy is a gift from the Spirit. He cannot give what He is not. That includes prophecy that we receive from others – it must be tested.

---

62  Mark Iles, School for Prophecy.

63  Proverbs 18:21; Deuteronomy 30:19.

64  See Esther chapter 8.

Walking a prophetic life, training further in prophecy, requires us to come to know who we believe, who we count as most precious, who we are, and courage to speak out. We fight a spiritual battle with our words of life and freedom, just by speaking them out from a position of authority as God's beloved son or daughter.

Queen Esther had come to her position not for her own benefit. She had to be prepared, body, soul and spirit, for her position. Then she had to know why she was there, why she could have an impact, and who would give her that favour and wisdom. Note that she listened to the suggestions of the advisors placed around her, and earned their favour. She also took only those simple things that were suggested to her into the king's presence when it was her turn, not the elaborate jewellery and decorations that the other girls probably took.

She had to submit and be teachable, receiving from those put in charge over her. She needed preparation to risk her life for her people, and wisdom was to be her guard. In the process, God became the victor over the enemy and His glory was shown. Many in the citadel of Susa converted to become Jews, through fear of the Lord. Simple obedience, devotion, and what Esther saw with her heart freed a nation and brought God's glory – only when she spoke out.

We too are to be honed, as Warriors of intimacy, developing ourselves and our hearts, and our relationship with the King of kings, over time.

Prophecy is a crucial vertebra in our backbone as believers in Jesus. Prophecy is clearly listed in the Bible as available to all believers if they want it.[65] We are encouraged by Paul[66] to eagerly desire prophecy. Who does not want to hear what the Father is saying to us more clearly? Who does not want to tell someone else by the Spirit, how they are seen in heaven?

Prophetic words received require testing, prayer and confirmation. This is helpful too for our faith level, for we are only to live by faith,[67] not by the prophecy or the one giving it. Testing the word and praying it back to God, talking to Him about it and hearing more on it from Him, will bring us to a place where we are actually standing on it by faith, as the Word from God for our lives.

This is teaching that has been sorely lacking in the Body of Christ,[68] which has dishonoured the biblical New Covenant prophetic gift, and the prophetic ministry, in the valuable part it should play in drawing out the gold in the people, churches, businesses, cities and nations around us. We need the prophetic ministry, and we need those prophets and prophetesses who understand their role in equipping 'his people for works of service, so that the

---

65   Mark Iles, School for Prophecy.

66   1 Corinthians 14:1.

67   Hebrews 11:6.

68   Teaching on this through Mark Iles, School for Prophecy; and Bethel Church, Redding, California; and Global Legacy (a ministry of Bethel Church).

body of Christ may be built up'.[69] Without them we are without vision and purpose.

A prophetic culture will bring freedom not restriction to the Body of Christ. It brings light into darkness, and 'adjusts the bones'.[70]

As we faithfully weigh, pray and speak out the prophecies given into our lives, the Holy Spirit breathes life into our faith. There is a process. The journey usually involves change, often loss of those things we once counted as important, and we become the people that we never expected to be!

Timothy was admonished in the above quote to meditate constantly on the words, because they would become reality in his life as he acted on them, thus bringing glory to God.

We become established in our future by using our prophetic words as a sword to cut away doubt and fear, and lies. We know what our Father has said to us, we have tested them and prayed them. Our backbone is strengthened and stretched, to carry the weight of what is to come. Others begin to see us as the Father sees us.

## Practical steps

Set a time when you will go through the words that have been spoken into your life. If there are none, ask God for

---

69  Ephesians 4:12.

70  Dr Jonathan Welton, *Equipping the Equippers* (Kindle, 2017).

some – seek some! He is faithful and He will give you them.

It is one of my learned disciplines to always record prophecy. I carry an iPhone, or a recorder around with me wherever I am. When I have recorded the word, I write it up immediately. I then print it out.

I go through it, testing it against Scripture, whether it points to Jesus, for any opinion or Old Covenant attitudes in it, for flavour of freedom. I take out the bits that do not pass the test. Over time, I take the word into God's presence, and according to the weight of the word, if it is directional, I ask Him for independent confirmation before I act. I take it to trusted advisors and review it.[71]

This process is precious, because it shows that we value what God speaks to us and wish to act on it. We get to spend time with God, hear more on what He might add to the word, and build our faith in the word so that we can stand on it, just as we would stand on Scripture, in faith. That way, we can use it to fight when times get tough. Otherwise, we are left in doubt with nothing to hold onto. It also means that we will be aware of anything that will need to change in our character or circumstances to reach fulfilment of the prophecy. Personal prophecies are conditional.

---

71   Mark Iles, School for Prophecy.

## THE POSTURE KEY:

Today, we are going to take three times once again, to do the simple stretching exercise which will loosen the muscles in your upper back, leaving them more flexible and therefore more comfortable in your work during the day:

- Sit upright on a chair, feet flat on the floor. Cross your arms over your chest like an X. Twist from your waist first to the left, hold briefly, then to the right, hold again. Repeat ten times each side. Keep your head as it would normally be in relation to your chest, don't twist your head round. Make sure your hips remain pointing forwards.

## THE STOPPING KEY:

- Find a tested prophetic word you have received and present it to God.

## THE BREATHING KEY:

- Breathe as we have been learning, from your diaphragm, whilst reminding yourself of the key highlighted words and phrases of that word.

## THE RELAXATION KEY:

Sit, or lie back, and be still to listen whilst continuing to breathe deeply from your diaphragm. Take what time you can – from five minutes upwards.

DAY
FIVE

# The Soaking Key

Try to set aside ten to thirty minutes today, in which you get comfortable, close your eyes, and do nothing except allow yourself to sink deep into God's love. Put on suitable music and let it happen. It can be useful to keep your notebook journal beside you and write down what you might hear in that time. Let Him encourage and establish your heart. We repeat this exercise twice a week, during which you will experience the power and security that comes from being in God's love.

DAY

SIX

# The Soaking Key

Get comfortable, close your eyes, and do nothing except allow yourself to sink deep into God's love again. Put on suitable music if you wish. Keep your notebook journal beside you and write down what you might hear in that time. Let Him encourage your heart and plant seeds of hope.

Check back and consider what you have learned and what you wish to establish in your life.

I recommend looking up in-depth teaching on prophecy. See Resources at the back of this book.

These are the vertebrae, the principles, we have looked at this week:

Protection

Preparation

Promise

Prophecy

This has been a week of Establishing.

## Prayer:

Abba, would You increase in us the desire to spend time in Your lap as dearly loved sons and daughters? Remind us of Your protection in that place, that You promise to prepare us by Your Holy Spirit, and that You purposefully give us Your very own words of encouragement through other sons and daughters, who prophesy your love. Thank You that Jesus opened the way for us to come so deeply into Your heart and discover the safe place where we can be truly ourselves.

Now, prepare to spend Day Seven with rest in our hearts.

Finish well, close to the heartbeat of God in partnership with Him, empowered by His Spirit and full of His peace.

# WEEK THREE

## Finishing

**PARTNERSHIP**

**PURSUE**

**POWER**

**PEACE**

# Partnership

We are not made to live and work alone but in fruitful partnership, each contributing who we are to the whole, worshipping the One in whom we have our life and who lives in each of us.

How many servants were present at the home in which Jesus was anointed by the woman with the costly vase? Were there other guests than the disciples? Her act, and Jesus' response, must have had a powerful effect on some of them. We do not know what happened to this woman afterwards. Using my imagination, I see her now with a following of those who saw the heart of what she did, and I see them working together to understand the fullness of what was revealed to them at that impacting moment.

I see her in her home, with others knocking at her door and being welcomed in to talk about her devotion and to wonder at its impact on Jesus. To talk about what this could mean for the future. I see her influencing her neighbourhood with the passion she held in her heart. I see others being gathered to the community of disciples, through the impact she had on them.

She was not living in a vacuum. She would have had connections, and those connections would have other connections. She would have seen Him as He died on the cross. She would have shared the news that He had risen again. She would have been a part of the day the Holy Spirit was poured out, and she would have finally understood the passion and the fire that had begun in her heart that history-making day she was with Jesus. We know her influence was about to be spread across the whole world.

That is all because she heard what Jesus said, not the criticism and down-talking of the disciples. It is vital that we listen to the right Voice. The devil has many voices, and so does our own head. We must drown those in the river of love that flows out of our Saviour's mouth.[72]

It is not possible to be in long-term fruitful partnership with other people unless we each learn how to become responsible for our own lives.[73] Unless we come to know

72  Beliefs Training is essential for the battle for your mind. Steve Backlund and Mark Iles' Resources are listed at the back of the book. See also Joyce Meyer's *Battlefield of the Mind* (Warner Faith, 2007).

73  See Danny Silk's training in Relationships, Boundaries (Bethel Church, Redding, California).

who we are in Christ, understand the royal privilege of being in His household and a part of His Bride, and His Body, we will have constant difficulties as the devil plants lie after lie in our heads.

Quite apart from that, there is power in gathering. We can pour all that we are on the feet of Jesus and on His head, all that we have and all that we know. When we do that *together*, the impact is phenomenal. When we worship the Lord of all the earth in unison, when we praise, dance, sing and love Him as one Body, we are affected by each member of that Body. When one worships extravagantly, that one member affects another member and the result is increase.

Who has not felt the increase in faith, hope and love when we are together in worship? It is the same when we bring our different gifts to the feet of Jesus. When we find our family, where we can be who we are in Jesus, we come home. We cannot fulfil the purpose God has for our life without our God-family, the Body. That is how God made us.

Just as each vertebra in our spine has ligaments running alongside and through it, with muscles to support and discs to separate one vertebra from the other, so we work together, live alongside, and worship in gathering together.[74] We are not called the Bride, and the Body, for nothing. Christianity has never been an individual

74   Ephesians 4:15-16.

pastime. For starters, it requires a living relationship with the Lord Jesus! And then, of course, He lives in constant relationship with the Holy Spirit, and His Father – who has many children!

It's in that place where we receive healing, where we come to understand and see Jesus, the Father and the Holy Spirit in ways we have never seen Him before. It's that way that God's glory will be revealed across the earth, and the way that it will be revealed to the principalities, and spiritual powers in the heavenly places.[75]

It is why apostles, prophets, evangelists, pastors, teachers too are to work in a team, together – we are not called to be lone rangers! We need one another – we even need several of each role to work together. The Kingdom has no hierarchy. We need to be different together, we need to keep an eye on each other, call one another's goodness out. Those we lead need different aspects of our roles in varying seasons in order to be built up and become mature. Or we become lopsided and topple over.

Ephesians 3:10-11 says: 'His intent was that now, through the church, the manifold wisdom of God should be made known to the rulers and authorities in the heavenly realms, according to his eternal purpose that he accomplished in Christ Jesus our Lord.'

---

75   Ephesians 3:10-11

## Practical steps

Begin to consider where you feel your family is. In order to posture ourselves for all that God wants to give us and to run the marathon well to the end, we need to be a living and active part of the Body of Christ. That means not only having the mindset that we are in a global family and a regional family, it means finding somewhere specific that becomes our family – and that does not need to be the closest geographically. God does not work only in certain denominations, either. Denomination is irrelevant. We gather around relationships. Take some time to deeply consider partnership and what kind of people you surround yourself with. See the Resources for teaching that will help you in the meantime. Ask God to help you find your people.

### THE POSTURE KEY:

- Sit on the edge of your chair with knees straight before you and feet flat on the ground. Physically draw your spine upwards. Reach your arms up and out, and push your shoulders down and back, whilst breathing in. Tilt your head back a little too. Feel the stretch in your thoracic spine. Hold for between fifteen and thirty seconds, breathing. Then relax and roll your shoulders up to your ears and backwards, a few times.

- Check the 'lordosis' in your lower back, that you have a curve forward there while you are sitting. Put a rolled-up towel behind your waist to help. Drop your shoulders down and a little back.

## THE STOPPING KEY:

- Pause in what you are doing. Lift your face to God for a moment.

## THE BREATHING KEY:

- Take some moments to breathe from your diaphragm, allowing your stomach to expand with the in-breath, and draw in with the out-breath. Breathe out longer than you breathe in.

## THE RELAXATION KEY:

- Lie flat on your back. Let your muscles relax. If necessary, put a small rolled-up towel underneath your waist, and a small cushion at your neck. Lie there for ten minutes with your eyes closed and let God minister to you – ask Him to send His Holy Spirit.

Then, ring a friend.

# Pursuit

It is in pursuit that we find. Stay hungry.

Pursuit is about passion. I am not talking of an everyday hobby or 'pursuit'. I am speaking of life-long, consistent, fierce, all-out passion to follow and to find. It means a flame that burns continuously brightly, and it needs fanning into flame.

This is a hunger for God that is never stilled, because the more we know Him and spend time with Him, the more we want of Him and His presence.

If the vertebra of pursuit is small and flaky then that is a weak link in our spiritual backbone, which means that our posture will be deformed.

Our attitude is to be dependent on God. I cannot write this book without the Holy Spirit. We cannot live our lives as He wants us to live them, without Him. We need His presence, His wisdom, His fruit. So often we think we can do it all without Him. We are human beings; we do think that. The key is to realise when that has happened and turn back to Him.

The Church in Laodicea was told: 'I know your deeds, that you are neither cold nor hot. I wish you were either one or the other!.'[76] It is not about our works, our performance, accomplishments, or successes and sacrifices. It is about passion! The Lord rebukes them as His loved ones, that they need to take a serious look at themselves and seek from Him what only He can give, for – listen to this – their lukewarmness was causing Him to vomit and spit them out. That sounds radical, but how much clearer can that be? This is truth said to loved ones, to help them to see![77] God is serious – He is a God of love, which means passion is involved. This 'rebuke' actually lifts a heavy yoke of performance and replaces it with joy – that is speaking truth in love, a Father who disciplines His children for their own good. If they did not listen, they would shrivel up with hard work. Our Father speaks to us kindly but clearly, for our benefit.

---

76   Revelation 3:15.

77   See Revelation 3:14-22.

Ignite the flame again. Go places to allow the flame of others to be the touchpaper. Get alone with Him and spend as much time as it needs to find Him again. Dig deep into the Word and meditate on it. Sing in tongues, speak in tongues around your house and in your day-to-day duties where you can.[78] Soak to suitable music.

Wield the prophecies spoken over you as a sword, when lies of doubt come knocking. In order to do that, you need to be sure that you have tested them for biblical accuracy, inner witness and then taken them into prayer to establish their content in your heart. Carry cards with you, with key points, just as it is wise to do with Scripture verses. Speak out!

Timothy is told by Paul: 'I'm writing to encourage you to fan into a flame and rekindle the fire of the spiritual gift God imparted to you when I laid my hands upon you.'[79] That does not sound tame, casual or lazy. In fact, the effect of this will be power, effectiveness and fruit in our lives: 'For God will never give you the spirit of cowardly fear, but he gives the Holy Spirit who gives you mighty power, love, and a mind that has been delivered, protected, and secure.'[80]

---

78  Our heavenly language: see 1 Corinthians 12-14.

79  2 Timothy 1:6, TPT.

80  2 Timothy 1:7, TPT.

Pursuit is not an option. He says, 'Seek My face.' Our reaction can be one or the other: having a heart response that connects with that phrase, allowing ourselves to be drawn into Him and letting His presence fill us, or seeing it float over our head and setting it aside for a better, more convenient, day.

Pursuit is sometimes like surfing a huge glistening wave following Jesus (who just happens to be walking on the water), with ease and passion and flow; or at times it can be like climbing a steep and rocky mountain, occasionally missing our footing or the path, and needing to stop and gain breath. Other times too He is hidden from view and we need to walk in fog by faith.

When we are about to move onto a new level in our lives, there is usually a time when God draws us more than normal, when we need to stoke up the flame more than we ever have done before. At these times, it is like coming before Him and waiting. Waiting. Then suddenly He comes and alights in our heart. Simple trust and waiting draw His heart to ours.

Contemplation, meditation, worship, praise, thanksgiving, the gift of tongues, soaking, are all disciplines we can use. Yet there is also the consistent practice of the values that He has taught us, learning and putting into our lives the principles that will stand us in good stead on the race. The battle for the mind is the spiritual warfare we must wage, capturing our thoughts to Jesus.

In the Song of Songs, there is a point at which the 'Bridegroom-King' draws her to a higher place. In The Passion Translation, He says: ' Arise, my dearest. Hurry, my darling. Come along with me! I have come as you have asked to draw you to my heart and lead you out. For now is the time, my beautiful one ... Arise, my love, my beautiful companion, and run with me to the higher place.'[81] We cannot be surprised when, once we have called out 'More Lord!', and pursued, that He answers and fully expects us to come to a higher place in Him. He continues in this passage to say that the little foxes must be caught that are spoiling the vineyard; these are the lies in our heads that prevent us from moving on – often the false humility we proudly retain.

The result in this passage is that fear and the fact that she does not feel ready stop her and she tells him to go on ahead and she will come away another time. He leaves. It is at this point that pursuit begins, for her. She finds that her heart can no longer rest as she let him go without her and she can no longer find him. She rises to search the city for him. When she finds him at last, she says, 'I caught

---

81   Song of Songs 2:10,13c, TPT.

him and fastened myself to him, refusing to be feeble in my heart again.'[82]

Those who have discovered their complete emptiness without the Lord are those who pursue and find Him. The race, the battle, is not for the strong, but for the weak who are transformed by His presence into glistening royal Warriors of intimacy.

## Practical steps

Take some of the practices I have mentioned above, and plan them into your life. For some of them, make appointments with yourself in your diary at regular intervals. Begin to cultivate the presence of God around your home and wherever you go, by keeping Him in mind, pursuing Him with your heart, and practising tongues, and singing in praise. This is not passive! It doesn't just happen. The more you cultivate this, the more you will feel the light in your heart that draws you to more.

Sometimes, I find that getting out of my seat to dance is an effort. I do not always feel like it. Yet when I have begun and I persist and I listen to the words of the worship music and use them in my heart, I find that my dance is interpreting those words, and I am lifting my heart to the Lord with a purity that is not my own. It is given to me, by Jesus, which makes me praise Him even more. It brings a

---

82   Song of Songs 3:4b, TPT.

reality to my life, that whatever I have done, I can always approach and pursue.

After those times, I carry a joy, and I am refreshed.

There was a period of time in my life when I read many small booklets containing readings by people such as Jean-Pierre de Caussade (a great eighteenth-century spiritual director), Jeanne Guyon (a woman interrogated by King Louis XIV and three Roman Catholic bishops for her 'heresy' and 'novel ideas'), Julian of Norwich, Brother Lawrence, *Thomas à Kempis* and more. This period brought me a sense of passion and pursuing God's presence. Reading widely and learning by 'chewing the meat and spitting out the bones' (Bill Johnson)[83] is a great way of developing your own posture before the Lord.

## THE POSTURE KEY:

- Posture yourself this time in worship. Stand up, stand before God. Feel your body upright and deliberately see yourself as a royal son or daughter.

## THE STOPPING KEY:

- Wait a moment more like this. Begin to tell your Father God how much you love Him.

83   Bethel Church, Redding, California.

## THE BREATHING KEY:

- Breathe as you begin to move in worship – you can dance, or you can bow, lift your hands, lie flat on your face. Try to get a rhythm of breathing throughout, moving slowly. Honour God with your body. Give Him your every breath.

## THE RELAXATION KEY:

- Sit or lie down, and imagine yourself curled up in your Father's lap. You are speaking to Him about what you have just experienced with Him.

DAY
THREE

# Power

Power holds a different meaning entirely when we look
at Jesus.

Power was wielded by the woman with the alabaster flask.
It was power to move Jesus' heart. The power of intense
gratitude, loss of concern about what people think, and
love flowed out of her onto Him just as the perfume
flowed. Forgiveness, healing and restitution became the
ointment that kept her sealed from the disciples' criticism
and disdain, as Jesus responded to her act.

The disadvantaged, the misaligned and the maladjusted
are those for whom Jesus gave His life. Those who felt
they were straight in line for the thrones when Jesus came
into what they thought would be His worldly kingdom,
were sorely disappointed.

The worldly power of earthly kingdoms was never a concern to Jesus and it still is not. After all, He puts in position every authority on earth. His focus is that the Kingdom of Heaven is brought to earth. He has already overcome, through His death on the cross. There will be a day when we see the fullness of that. In the meantime, it is we who are called to bring the Kingdom of Heaven to earth wherever we are.[84]

This means that how we behave will be in direct conflict with the world. We are not part of the world. We are part of the Kingdom of Heaven now that we have given our lives to Jesus. I have already described Jesus' Kingdom to be upside down – it is a place where leaders serve. Not everybody is going to understand this. We must be ready to stand out whatever the cost.

Power in this Kingdom is, therefore, not the same as power in the world.

We carry a weight of glory because Jesus lives within us. This is not our own. We are given His seal of authority and we act on His behalf and in His name. This weight of glory is to cover the earth. Just one of us cannot cover the earth. We need many of us. So, in God's Kingdom, we empower. We spread the glory. We build people around

---

84    Read Bill Johnson's *When Heaven Invades Earth* (Destiny Image, 2013).

us to be big.[85] We do not wield power as a weapon, we spread power by empowering.[86]

Jesus expressed great power in meekness. He carried presence, and demons would flee in that presence. They recognised power and authority running through Him. He did not need to shout at them. He quietly stands up in the synagogue at Nazareth, to read out what He has come to do:

> The Spirit of the LORD is upon Me,
>
> Because He has anointed Me
>
> To preach the gospel to the poor;
>
> He has sent Me to heal the brokenhearted,
>
> To proclaim liberty to the captives
>
> And recovery of sight to the blind,
>
> To set at liberty those who are oppressed;
>
> To proclaim the acceptable year of the LORD.

Then he sits down and announces, 'Today this Scripture is fulfilled in your hearing.'[87] It was customary to stand while reading, and to sit down when teaching. Sitting down added an authority and a prophetic fulfilment to His words.

---

85   'My goal is not to build a big church, but to build big people.' Bill Johnson, Bethel Church, Redding, California.

86   Read Steve Buckland's *The Culture of Empowerment* (Steve Backlund, 2016).

87   Luke 4:16-30, NKJV.

The ripples that sent through the gathering can be felt even now as we read it. Yet it does not seem to ruffle Him when they become angry at Him, and seek to throw Him off the cliff. He is described as passing through the midst of them and going on His way! That needed supernatural intervention, overcoming worldly authority, quietly and easily.

Jesus knew who He was when He formed a whip and chased the money-lenders out of the temple.[88] He spoke the truth, He lived by His values, and He feared no man. When He taught, we see that people were 'astonished at His teaching, for His word was with authority'.[89] It is not about great learning and intellect, it is about Who we know, and who we know we are.

His power came through because His identity was sure. He knew who He was. We cannot be Warriors in God's Kingdom without a true understanding of our identity. Without this, we will not be able to wield the sword of service in leadership, when we put on our apron, fill the water bowl, take the towel and wash the feet of those we lead. That is power. Weakness is power because it is turned into strength by dependence on God.

Paul writes to the Corinthians about Jesus: 'But for those who have been chosen to follow him, both Jews and Greeks, he is God's mighty power, God's true wisdom, and our Messiah. For the "foolish" things of God have

---

88  John 2:15.

89  Luke 4:32, NKJV.

proven to be wiser than human wisdom. And the "feeble" things of God have proven to be far more powerful than any human ability.'[90]

## Practical steps

We are once again on the third day of our week, when I talk about taking exercise!

There are many types of exercise, as you know – walking is only one suggestion. My husband finds that he can process his thoughts, come up with ideas, and spend time with God while he is on the running machine in the gym, swimming in the pool, or cycling his road-bike around the Wiltshire countryside. He comes home refreshed, refocused and alert, ready for the day, or well-processed to allow his mind to sleep at night.

I have learned to incorporate several types of exercise into my week. I too find that processing thoughts, focusing on some ideas and thinking into them, and worshipping God while on the cross-trainer in the gym, or swimming, is great. I do indeed value the times when I may sit quietly doing nothing and contemplating God, or meditating on Scripture, yet this active way is an additional suggestion and you can weave it into a fitness programme.

God is interested in your body and soul as well as your spirit! He doesn't mind being 'woven in' to your day or your fitness regime! In fact, He revels in it. Sometimes I

---

90  1 Corinthians 1:24-25, TPT.

can literally feel Him catching up with me – or me with Him when I am out walking – and beginning to talk with me, or just be with me and I with Him. When I am out on my mountain bike bouncing across the bridle-paths and cross-country, I feel Him showing me things with delight – birds, views, sunrises, clouds. When I take my camera, He shows me the detail in a rock, or the patterns in the sand.

You will find that keeping healthily active will empower you. After all, your body is the temple of the Holy Spirit. He lives in you. Our bodies need to carry Him well to the end of our days, and our souls – mind, will, emotions – also cry out to be submitted to His care. See David's example in the Psalms!

## THE POSTURE KEY:

- Look back at the stretches I have given you in this book. Consider how you will incorporate them into your days. There are more too – look them up on the internet. Today though, I want you to go to a mirror and look at yourself.

## THE STOPPING KEY:

- Pause and thank God for who you see in the mirror.

## THE BREATHING KEY:

- Breathe as I have taught you, from your diaphragm. Listen for your Father's voice as you keep looking at yourself in your eyes. For some of you, this may be difficult. Persist. You are wonderfully made.

## THE RELAXATION KEY:

- Now close your eyes and thank Him that He is going to help you to find ways of living your days with body, soul and spirit power, through His Holy Spirit, and that He will help you find ways of nourishing all three areas of yourself. You will be confident and bold.

If you have time, read and soak in Psalm 139:1-18,23-24. Make a decision to look after yourself. This does not mean slavery to diets. It means simply letting God love you, teach you; and keeping active, eating well.[91]

---

91  Beni Johnson has written a helpful book on this subject, see Resources.

DAY
FOUR

# Peace

And the peace of God, which transcends all understanding, will guard your hearts and your minds in Christ Jesus.
Philippians 4:7

Peace is the final vertebra in the spiritual thoracic spine, joining it to the lumbar vertebrae below the ribs. Therefore, it is at the core of all we do. Peace is the atmosphere of the Kingdom, where striving is counterproductive.

Many strive to fight to gain the Kingdom when Jesus has already won it for us through the cross. The Kingdom is within us because Jesus is within us. Paul tells the Ephesians 'For our struggle is not against flesh and blood, but against the rulers, against the authorities, against the powers of this dark world and against the spiritual forces of evil in the heavenly realms.'[92] This requires different

92   Ephesians 6:12.

weapons. The most important of those is peace. Peace can overcome in the most difficult of situations.

Yet we actually need to contend for our peace! It requires acting in the opposite spirit. At times, it requires our stepping back in to Jesus, out of the situation we find ourselves in. It requires keeping our mouth shut, or saying something that builds someone up who has just torn us down. It requires waiting before acting.

We need to let go and let God come in and *be* peace within us. It is a fruit of the Spirit. Which means that if the Spirit is in us, the fruit is in us already. It is about receiving and believing, and deliberately using self-control – another fruit of the Spirit – to pause, before acting. It takes practise!

I love that this is our last vertebra in the book. It seals everything. Without peace, we cannot live the Christian life. We are called to peace.[93] The Kingdom of God is righteousness, peace and joy in the Holy Spirit.[94]

The Philippians quote at the start of this section follows instructions to rejoice always, in everything to rejoice, to let people see our gentleness, knowing that the Lord is at hand! We are instructed not to be anxious about anything, rather, to pray and ask God, thanking Him and letting our requests be known to Him. *Then* we will know the peace of God, and that peace will guard

---

93  Colossians 3:15.

94  Romans 14:17.

our hearts from the turmoil of emotions, and stand guard over our minds to keep them from the torment of lies and faulty thinking. This will also keep our spirit at peace, filling it with a joy and a rest beyond what our mind can comprehend.

Peace can be when you left home in very good time, you are in a traffic jam on the way to the airport that in the natural will not clear before you need to check in, but you know that the Holy Spirit is telling you that you will get there in time for your flight. Easy to hold that peace? No, because what you are seeing with your eyes tells you otherwise. Yet as you strengthen your faith in what God has spoken to you, and you ask Jesus to be peace within you, you find that peace increases each time, and you find that He acts on your behalf where you cannot see a way. That is one of our own testimonies!

Peace is letting the situation go to God. Literally handing it over to Him in your imagination. Then waiting for His answer.

Peace is holding His presence within you all day, training yourself to recognise it, and consciously resting in His peace.

Peace is knowing the truth of Romans 8:37-39: '[I]n all these things we overwhelmingly conquer through Him who loved us. For I am convinced that neither death, nor life, nor angels, nor principalities, nor things present, nor things to come, nor powers, nor height, nor depth, nor any other created thing, will be able to separate us from the love of God, which is in Christ Jesus our Lord.'[95]

It is my learning process. We are called to do everything out of a place of 'rest'. That means, everything we do must come from peace in God, knowing who we are in Him, recognising Him for who He is, knowing that it is well with our soul because He is there for us and has won the victory on the cross. Doing everything out of a place of rest does not mean we are physically resting all of the time.

Peace is knowing the Father has run to embrace us, put the robe and the ring on us, sandals on our feet and brought us into His household as His son. He is throwing a party for us and we can sit back and enjoy it. We do not have to strive like the older son. We do not have to allow the older son's attitude to infect our peace.[96] We just need to know and receive the love of the Father. That is what makes us royal Warriors. It is all about grace.

Surrendering into the arms of grace, the arms of the Father, is where we find infinite peace, nourishment and all that we need.

---

95   NASB.

96   The prodigal son – see Luke 15.

## Practical steps

It is time to surrender. Go to the mirror again. Draw your body up straight, look yourself in the eye, and tell yourself that it is Time. Tell yourself that you are a beloved child of your Father God. Tell yourself that you are free.

### THE POSTURE KEY:

Now take this posture of body, soul and spirit that I and the prayer ministers developed in the Healing Rooms at Bethel one Saturday, as a fun expressive idea with powerful, memorable effects:

Look yourself in the eyes.

Put your hand on your chest and say:

'I submit my spirit to the Holy Spirit.'

Each time you say, 'to the Holy Spirit', bring both arms upwards and touch your hands together.

Put your hand on your forehead (mind), chest (will), and stomach (emotions) for each of the following, saying:

'I submit my mind, will and emotions to my spirit, which is submitted to the Holy Spirit.

(Once again bring both arms upwards and touch your hands together on 'submitted to the Holy Spirit'.)

Now move your hands in the air over your head, and

down each side of your body to your feet, as you say the following:

'I submit my body to my spirit, which is submitted to the Holy Spirit.'

Stand back up to once again move both hands upwards and touch them together above your head to signify the Holy Spirit.

Now you have activated this, you are reminded that your peace comes from being submitted to the Holy Spirit, and therefore allowing your own spirit to lead your soul and body, rather than permitting your mind, will, emotions, or body, to lead you.

## THE STOPPING KEY:

- At three points today, stop whatever you are doing and close your eyes, and turn your face up to Jesus. Remind yourself that you are His. That you are constantly on His heart.

## THE BREATHING KEY:

- Spend some moments breathing as we have been learning, from your diaphragm.

## THE RELAXATION KEY:

- Put some music on and dance! Or use one of the suggestions on the list at the end of this book.

DAY FIVE

# The Soaking Key

Plan to set aside thirty minutes today in which to soak in God's presence. Put worship music on, get comfortable, close your eyes, and do nothing except allow yourself to sink deep into God's love. Yes, you might fall asleep, but that's OK. It can be useful to keep your notebook journal beside you and write down what you might hear in that time, once you have finished soaking.

Often you feel more refreshed, more alive and ideas flow, after a time of soaking. The time spent seems to pay for itself. Yet the most important outcome is that you get to relax with God, the Creator of the universe – your Father, the Lord Jesus and the Holy Spirit. If you think about it, that's quite a community!

# The Soaking Key

Today, begin by reading the allegory, *Eagle Wing* a couple of times. Mull it over and let God speak to you through it.

Then put on some worship music, get comfortable, close your eyes and soak in the Holy Spirit while He tends to you. Use thirty minutes if you can, otherwise whatever you can manage.

Journal your thoughts when you are finished, and what you may have heard or experienced.

Soaking is a great practice to keep going through your life. Plan in times for it.

These are the vertebrae, the principles, we have looked at this week:

Partnership

Pursue

Power

Peace

The week has been about Finishing.

## Prayer:

Father, as we walk out into our lives with these principles in our hearts, help us to understand that You are with us and will never leave us. Draw us deeper and speak to us more strongly. Send us people who can run the race with us, to finish well.

Now, prepare to spend Day Seven with rest in our hearts.

Bless you on your onward journeys! Do send me testimonies – you will find my email address at the back.

Spend some time with the allegory on the following page, and see what the Father wants to tell you. Let it encourage you.

# EAGLE WING

Eagle Wing dimmed the cheering voices as she stepped to the starting line. Bare-footed as was the culture of her country, she was sure and fleet of foot and ready for the marathon lying before her. Mapped out in her head she could revise every twist and turn, but her success depended upon the force of energy and guidance within her that was the Holy Spirit of her God.

Breathing deeply and focusing her vision on the distance, she took her place amongst the crowd of runners. No kneeling at a starting block as in a sprint, bunched up ready to shoot out of the starting position, extend herself a short distance and touch the finishing line – for her, this would be a race of endurance. Endurance she had learned over a long time of discipline, falling and picking herself back up, learning from her mistakes.

Her God had taught her as they walked and ran in the fields. Her feet had been bruised and had needed healing. He had left his throne – for He was a King – to tend to her. He had bathed them, washed them, and tended them until they were steady, strong and fast. This was the nature of the Kingdom she came from. He had talked to her often, as they relaxed while the evenings drew in, about the marathon that was to come. Gradually her understanding grew until one day she felt confident in her ability and empowered to run her race.

The runners around her now, pushing and jostling for position, were all wearing the best trainers. They all seemed taller than her, but she was not daunted. She had been taught her worth, her ability and her identity as a King's daughter. Her name described the strength and power of her identity, the ability to soar above all difficulties and the impact she had when flying in her gift. It also signified the freedom of her land and its culture. She was a first-time runner in this marathon, a marathon to the end, but she was confident and expectant. Fear would come and face her as he always did – but she had been taught to look beyond him, outface him or ignore him. And now the day had come, for the real race.

# CONCLUSION

We are born to make the dark places afraid by love.
We have a different Spirit.

Unexpected Warriors are those who do not win by strength, fame or qualification. They win because Jesus won for them, and they have been set free to become the real children of God they were created to be. Daily they use weapons that are not of this world, that seem soft, but are packed full of resurrection power, power to raise people from the dead to live lives to set free. They win, by standing.

Unexpected Warriors are also those who never expected to have a voice. They are those who were hidden who have come to light. They have been lit by the touchpaper of God, breathed into by His breath so that they discover who they really are.

We have seen that the woman who broke the vase of perfume over Jesus did not only do that. She broke the religious spirit of her age and of ours. She was an Unexpected Warrior. We have seen Queen Esther speak up for the freedom of her people, risking her own life in the process. She too was an Unexpected Warrior. We have seen Stephen, dying by stoning, forgiving the stoners, seeing a vision of Jesus while he died, and showing us peace in persecution. He too was an Unexpected Warrior.

Caleb was described as having 'a different spirit'.[97] He and Joshua saw possibility when the rest of the spies saw impossibility.[98] Both retained this attitude throughout their lives. They knew the value of what they possessed, their relationship with God and what He had promised to them, and for that they were ready to fight.

We are being called out of our wilderness and being given a voice, to be bold. We train for the marathon, not the short sprint. Our bones are oiled with joy. We do not compare ourselves to others and we recognise that the Holy Spirit within us overcomes all weakness. We lean on Him. It is up to Jesus to finish what He has started in us, as He promised. Flex the backbone you have been given, test the vertebrae and renew your mind to believe. Get to the starting line knowing you have won the race already. And have fun!

---

97   Numbers 14:24.

98   See Numbers 13:26-33; Joshua 14:6-15.

Most of all, recognise your freedom! Remind yourself regularly that 'Freedom is the end game',[99] and that we have been called to be children, and our Father is God.

So, as Paul says to the Corinthians, 'May joyous grace and endless peace be yours continually from our Father God and from our Lord Jesus, the Anointed One.'[100]

---

99    Mark Iles, School for Prophecy.

100    1 Corinthians 1:3, TPT.

# ACTIVITIES AND RELAXATION SUGGESTIONS

Dance – not just for worship – sometimes use this for 'breakout' times! Remember King David danced 'with all his might'[101] before the Lord!

Sing – or shout. That is biblical too.

Walk

Swim

Cycle

Run

Colour

Paint

Sketch

Make something

Do part of a jigsaw puzzle

Read part of a book or magazine

---

101   2 Samuel 6:14.

Repot a plant

Prune a rose

Walk round the garden and notice each plant

Wander around your house and consider each room or just one room

Think in a focused manner on something

Thank God

Praise, using a psalm

Worship using your body to interpret what you are saying/feeling

Listen to music

Write something

Take a ten-minute nap

Get out to the beach on a windy day

Get up a hill and pray

Sit on a rock on the coastline or on a tree trunk in a wood, look and listen

Take ten minutes' silence, eyes closed; focus on Jesus or a Bible verse

Bible meditation, chew a verse slowly and repeatedly. On tough days, set your mobile phone or watch alarm on every hour, and stop to thank God for something.

# RECOMMENDED RESOURCES

Mark Iles, *School for Prophecy courses:*
(schoolforprophecy@gmail.com)
*Developing Your Prophetic Gift, Level 1*
*Growing a Prophetic Ministry, Level 2*

## Books

Iles, Mark, *Developing Your Prophetic Gift, School for Prophecy Level 1 Course Manual* (Onwards and Upwards 2018)

Iles, Mark, *Growing A Prophetic Ministry, School for Prophecy Level 2 Course Manual* (Due for publication in 2019)

Backlund, Steve, *Cracks in the Foundation* (Steve Backlund, 2014)

Backlund, Steve, *Possessing Joy* (Igniting Hope, 2012)

Backlund, Steve, *The Culture of Empowerment* (Steve Backlund, 2016)

Johnson, Beni, 40 Days to Wholeness, Body, Soul and Spirit (Destiny Image, 2016).

Johnson, Bill, *When Heaven Invades Earth* (Destiny Image, 2013)

Leaf, Dr Caroline, *Switch On Your Brain*, Baker 2015

Silk, Danny, *Culture of Honor* (Destiny Image, 2013).

Silk, Danny, *Keep Your Love On* (Loving on Purpose, 2015)

Vallotton, Kris, *Destined to Win* (Thomas Nelson, 2017)

Vallotton, Kris, *Spirit Wars* (Chosen Books, 2012)

Song of Songs, The Passion Translation

The Book of Esther, the Bible

## Websites

Bethel Church, Redding, California: www.ibethel.org

Kris Vallotton: kvministries.com

Steve and Wendy Backlund: www.ignitinghope.com

## Album

Wendy Backlund, *Encounter: An Activation of Your Spirit*

## Healing

Sozo Ministries: www.bethelsozo.com

In UK: www.bethelsozo.org.uk

# ABOUT THE AUTHOR

Richard and Martina have been married for thirty-two years and have two adult sons. They have an armed forces background of thirty years together. They are committed members of the family at Winchester Vineyard church, UK.

Martina is in the prophetic ministry, a member of Southampton-based School for Prophecy. She has ministered with Mark Iles and the team for almost five years, and in Vineyard churches.

She has 23 years' experience in the anglican church, out of which she brought her heart to bring identity, freedom, release and deliverance into people's lives, often expressed using artistic impression.

You can reach her at
www.nantenterprises.com/grace-creativity

Lightning Source UK Ltd.
Milton Keynes UK
UKHW02f0608181217
314659UK00005B/98/P